Treasury of
COUNTRY
COOKING AND CRAFTS

PUBLICATIONS INTERNATIONAL, LTD.

CREDITS

Craft Designers: Sarah Achterof (page 90); Lori Blankenship (pages 80, 163); Judy Gibbs/Hollie Designs (pages 85, 123, 152); Trena Hegdahl (page 184); Janet Immordino (pages 42, 94, 98, 106, 138, 189); Vicki Schweitzer (pages 26, 46, 57, 142, 173); Carol Spooner (pages 34, 50, 52, 74); Dee Dee Triplett (pages 20, 116); Retta Warehime (pages 64, 110, 155); Kathy Wirth (pages 101, 127, 135); Ricë Freeman-Zachery (page 170)

Food Stylist: Carol Parik

Technical Advisor: Brenda Coppola

Photography: Peter Dean Ross

Other Photography: Burke/Triolo Productions; Chris Cassidy; Sacco Productions Limited/Chicago; Sanders Studios, Inc.

Photo Credits: FPG International: William H. Clark: 136, Richard Johnston: 61, William McKinney: 72-73, Ron Thomas: 18-19, 21, Arthur Tilley: 107; International Stock: Wayne Aldridge: 126, Bob Firth: 95, 104-105, 142, Phyllis Picardi: 117, Tom Till: 140-141; Photri, Inc.: 43, 47, 53, 154, W. Biedel, M.D.: Table of contents (top right & bottom left), 144; Rainbow: 35, Bill Binzen: 172, Dan McCoy: 134, 190, Hank Morgan: Back cover (bottom); Super-Stock: 99, 111, 139.

Photo Stylist: Sally Grimes

Model: Theresa Lesniak/Royal Model Management

Photo Sites: Bonnie Garrett, Becky & Pate Gustafson, Eileen Murphy, Terri & Paul Schroeder

Product Acknowledgements: Kunin Felt, Hampton, NH

The publisher gratefully acknowledges the kind permission granted to reprint the following copyrighted material. Should any copyright holder have been inadvertently omitted they should apply to the publisher who will be pleased to credit them in full in any subsequent editions.

Lines from *The Age of Innocence:* Reprinted with permission of Scribner, an imprint of Simon & Schuster, Inc. from THE AGE OF INNOCENCE by Edith Wharton. Copyright 1920 D. Appleton and Company. Copyright renewed 1948 by William R. Tyler.

Pictured on front cover: (clockwise, starting at top left) Gingerbread Pear Muffins (page 162), Fall Harvest Wreath (page 189), Best Ever Apple Pie (page 132), Fuzzie Bear (page 46), Basic White Bread (page 79), Country Scents Quilt (page 155).

Table of Contents

CRAFT TECHNIQUES *page 6*

Craft Techniques

Crafting Techniques

What is more country than crafting? Nothing! You can make the wonderful projects in this book as gifts or add to your home decor. The *Treasury of Country Cooking and Crafts* offers you many exciting crafts that take a day or less to create. Things made by hand come from the heart!

The projects in this book include a wide variety of techniques and methods. Take a moment and look through the pages. You'll find everything from traditional counted cross-stitch to rubber stamping. We hope you enjoy creating these projects. They are for all skill levels and interests.

Before plunging into your chosen project, read the directions thoroughly. Check to make sure you have all the materials needed. Being prepared will make your project easier and more enjoyable.

Next, read the basic information in the pages that follow for the craft you're doing. These pages will help you choose materials, will define terms, and will describe certain techniques that are essential to that craft.

Using Patterns

Enlarging patterns: Many of the patterns in this book are printed smaller than actual size in order to fit them on the page. You will have to enlarge them before using them. You can do this on a photocopier, copying the pattern at the percentage indicated. If you don't have access to a photocopier, you can use the grid method.

To use the grid method, you will need graph paper or other paper ruled in one-inch squares. The first step is to draw a grid of evenly spaced lines over the pattern in the book. The next step is to copy, square by square, the pattern from the smaller grid in the book to the one-inch graph paper. Using the grid ensures that the pattern is enlarged proportionately.

The size of the grid you draw on the pattern depends on the degree of enlargement you need. If the pattern is to be 200 percent of what is in the book, your grid will consist of ½-inch squares. If the pattern is to be copied at 150 percent, the squares in your grid will be two-thirds of an inch.

Transferring patterns: Once your pattern is the correct size, you can use it as directed in the project instructions. One method is to transfer a pattern to another surface by tracing over the lines of the pattern with an iron-on transfer pen. Follow the manufacturer's directions to iron the pattern onto the surface. You can also use transfer paper, which comes in various colors. Sandwich the transfer paper between the pattern and the surface.

Cross-Stitch

Cross-stitch is traditionally worked on an "even-weave" cloth that has vertical and horizontal threads of equal thickness and spacing. Six-strand embroidery floss is used for most stitching; there are also many beautiful threads that can be used to enhance the appearance of the stitching.

Basic Supplies

Fabric: The most common even-weave fabric is 14-count Aida cloth. The weave of this fabric creates distinct squares that make stitching very easy for the beginner.

But you can work on any cloth, such as linen, just keep your stitches consistent and even.

Needles, hoops, and scissors: A blunt-end or tapestry needle is used for counted cross-stitch. A #24 needle is the recommended size for stitching on 14-count Aida cloth. You may use an embroidery hoop while stitching—just be sure to remove it when not working on your project. A small pair of sharp scissors are a definite help when working with embroidery floss.

Floss: Six-strand cotton embroidery floss is most commonly used, and it's usually cut into 18-inch lengths for stitching. Follow instructions for the project you choose. Commonly, two of the six strands are used for stitching on 14-count Aida cloth and two strands are used for backstitching.

To locate the center of the design, lightly fold your fabric in half and in half again. Find the center of the chart by following the arrows on the sides.

Each square on the chart equals one stitch on the fabric. The colors correspond to the floss numbers listed in the color key. Select a color and stitch all of that color within an area. Begin by holding the thread ends behind the fabric until secured or covered over with two or three stitches. You may skip a few stitches on the back of the material, but do not run the thread from one area to another behind a section that will not be stitched in the finished piece—it will show through the fabric. If your thread begins to twist, drop the needle and allow the thread to untwist. To end a thread, weave or run the thread under several stitches on the back side. Cut the ends close to the fabric.

Each counted cross-stitch is represented by a colored square on the project's chart. For horizontal rows, work the stitches in two steps, i.e., all of the left to right stitches and then all of the right to left stitches (see Figure A). For vertical rows, work each complete stitch as shown in Figure B. Three-quarter stitches are often

used when the design requires two colors in one square or to allow more detail in the pattern (see Figure C). The backstitch is often used to outline or create letters, and is shown by bold lines on the patterns. Backstitch is usually worked after the pattern is completed (see Figure D).

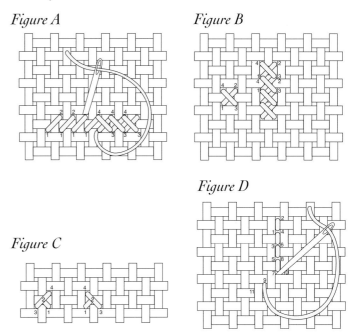

Figure A

Figure B

Figure C

Figure D

Plastic Canvas

Plastic canvas allows for three-dimensional stitchery projects to be constructed. Plastic canvas is easy to do, easy on the eyes, and easy on the pocketbook, too.

Basic Supplies

Plastic canvas: Canvas is most widely available by the sheet. Stitch all the pieces of a project on the same brand of plastic canvas to ensure that the meshes will match when you join them together.

Plastic canvas comes in several counts or mesh sizes (number of stitches to the inch) and numerous sizes of sheets. Specialty sizes and shapes such as circles are also available. Most canvas is clear, although up to 24 colors are available. Colored canvas is used when parts of the project remain unstitched. Seven-count canvas comes in four weights—standard; a thinner flexible weight; a stiffer, rigid weight; and a softer weight made especially for bending and curved projects. Designs can be stitched on any mesh count—the resulting size of the project is the only thing that will be affected. The smaller the count number, the larger the project will be.

Needles: Needle size is determined by the count size of the plastic canvas you are using. Patterns generally call for a #18 needle for stitching on 7-count plastic canvas, a #16 or #18 for 10-count canvas, and a #22 or #24 for stitching on 14-count plastic canvas.

Yarns: A wide variety of yarns may be used. The most common is worsted weight (or 4-ply). Acrylic yarns are less expensive and washable; wool may also be used. Several companies produce specialty yarns for plastic canvas work. These cover the canvas well and will not "pill" as some acrylics do. Sport weight yarn (or 3-ply) and embroidery floss are often used on 10-count canvas. Use 12 strands or double the floss thickness for 10-count canvas and 6 strands for stitching on 14-count canvas. On 14-count plastic canvas, many of the specialty metallic threads made for cross-stitch can be used to highlight and enhance your project.

Cutting Out Your Project

Many plastic canvas projects are dimensional—a shape has to be cut out and stitched. Scissors or a craft knife are recommended.

Preparing to Stitch

Cut your yarn to a 36-inch length. Begin by holding the yarn end behind the fabric until secured or covered over with two or three stitches. To end a length, weave or run the yarn under several stitches on the back side. Cut the end close to the canvas. The continental stitch is the most commonly used stitch to cover plastic canvas. Decorative stitches will add interest and texture to your project. As in cross-stitch, if your yarn begins to twist, drop

the needle and allow the yarn to untwist. Do not pull your stitches too tight, since this causes gaps in your stitching and allows the canvas to show. Also do not carry one color yarn across too many rows of another color on the back—the carried color may show through to the front of your project. Do not stitch the outer edge of the canvas until the other stitching is complete. If the project is a single piece of canvas, overcast the outer edge with the color specified. If there are two or more pieces, follow the pattern instructions for assembly.

Cleaning

If projects are stitched with acrylic yarn, they may be washed by hand using warm or cool water and a mild detergent. Place on a terry cloth towel to air dry. Do not place in a dryer or dry clean.

The following stitches are used in plastic canvas:

Backstitch
Work the plastic canvas backstitch just as you do a cross-stitch backstitch.

Continental Stitch
For the continental stitch, your needle comes up at 1 and all odd-numbered holes and goes down at 2 and all even-numbered holes.

Slanting Gobelin Stitch
For the slanting gobelin stitch, your needle comes up at 1 and all odd-numbered holes and goes down at 2 and all even-numbered holes.

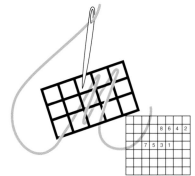

French Knot

For the French knot, bring your needle up at a hole and wrap yarn clockwise around needle. Holding the yarn, insert needle in the hole to the right and slowly pull yarn.

Overcast Stitch

For the overcast stitch, the needle goes down at the numbered holes, and the yarn wraps over the edge of the canvas. Make sure to cover the canvas completely.

Ribbon Embroidery

Ribbon embroidery is much like regular embroidery or crewel work, except you use silk or silklike ribbon instead of yarn or floss. Be careful to keep ribbon untwisted as you work. You will work much looser stitches than in traditional embroidery. A few practice stitches will show you how easy embroidery with ribbon is!

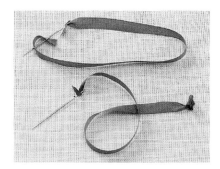

Cut ribbon to 12- to 14-inch lengths, angle-cutting the ends of the ribbon. Thread the ribbon through the eye of the needle and, about ½ inch from one end, pierce through the center of the ribbon with the needle. Pull the other end of ribbon until the ribbon "locks" into place.

To knot the end of the ribbon, double the very end of the ribbon and pierce the end with the point of the needle. Pull the ribbon through, forming a knot.

To finish stitching, either tie off ribbon next to the fabric or make a few small backstitches and trim the tail. If you plan on washing your finished project, use a drop of washable glue to keep ribbon from fraying.

The following are the stitches used in this book:

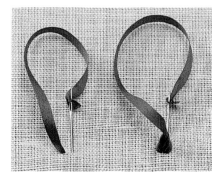

Lazy Daisy

Bring needle and thread up and hold ribbon with your finger on top of fabric. Being sure not to twist ribbon, reinsert needle next to the entry hole to make a loop. Bring needle up at inside end of loop and go over top of loop and insert needle at outside end of loop.

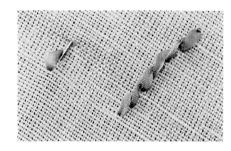

Stem Stitch

Keeping ribbon untwisted, work from left to right making even, small stitches. Come up in the middle of the first stitch and down half the length past the end of the first stitch. Repeat stitching for length indicated.

Japanese Ribbon Stitch

Bring needle and ribbon up and lay ribbon on fabric. Keeping ribbon flat, insert needle at end of stitch. Pull needle through to back of fabric.

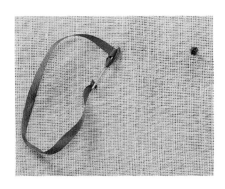

French Knot

Bring needle and ribbon up through fabric. Wrap ribbon around needle twice and reinsert needle next to starting point. Slowly pull needle through ribbon.

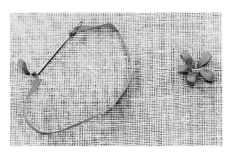

Loop Flower

Form loops by bringing needle and ribbon up and reinserting needle next to starting point. Keep ribbon untwisted and leave enough ribbon loop to create a petal. While making next loop, be sure to hold first loop so you don't pull it through. Continue making five loops to create flower.

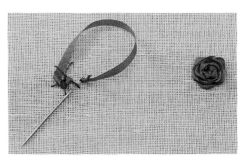

Spider Web Rose

Use embroidery floss to make a five-spoked star. Thread needle with ribbon and bring needle and ribbon up at middle of star. Weave ribbon over and under star points to create rose.

Decorative Wood Painting

Decorative painting has been handed down from generation to generation. It's an art form that was developed by untrained artists and no artistic talent or drawing skills are necessary.

Wood Preparation

Properly preparing your wood piece can make all the difference in the outcome. Having a smooth surface to work on will allow you to complete the project quickly and easily. Once the wood is prepared, you are ready to proceed with a basecoat, stain, or finish, according to the project instructions. Some finishes, such as crackling, will recommend not sealing the wood. Always read instructions completely before starting.

Supplies: Sand paper (#200) for removing roughness; tack cloth, which is a sticky resin-treated cheesecloth, to remove dust after sanding; a wood sealer to seal wood and prevent warping; and a foam or 1-inch flat brush to apply sealer. Note: Wood with knot holes requires a special sealer to prevent sap from later bleeding through the paint. Check the manufacturer's label for proper usage.

Basic Painting Techniques

Thin lines

1. Thin paint with 50 percent water for a fluid consistency that flows easily off the brush. It should be about ink consistency. Use a liner brush for short lines and tiny details and a script brush for long lines. Dip brush into thinned paint. Wipe excess on palette.

2. Hold brush upright with handle pointing to the ceiling. Use your little finger as a balance when painting. Don't apply pressure for extra thin lines.

Floating Color

This technique is also called side loading. It is used to shade or highlight the edge of an object. Floated color is a gradual blend of color to water.

1. Moisten an angle or flat brush with water. Blot excess water from brush, setting bristles on paper towel until shine of water disappears. Dip the long corner of brush into paint. Load paint sparingly. Carefully stroke brush on palette until color blends halfway across the brush. If the paint blends all the way to short side, clean and load again.

2. Hold the brush at a 45 degree angle, and using a light touch, apply color to designated area.

Splattering

Splattering is when little dots of paint are sprinkled on the surface. This technique is great for creating snow, aged fly spec look, or just adding fun colors to a finish. Always test splattering on paper first.

1. Thin paint with 50 to 80 percent water. Use an old toothbrush and palette knife or a Kemper tool. Dip brush into thinned paint. Lots of paint on the brush will create large dots. As paint runs out, dots become finer.

2. When using a toothbrush, drag your thumb or palette knife across the top of the bristles, causing them to bend. As you release, the bristles spring forward, splattering the paint onto the surface. With a Kemper tool, hold brush over object and twist handle.

Dots

Perfect round dots can be made with any round implement. The size of the implement determines the size of the dot. You can use the wooden end of a brush, a stylus tip, a pencil tip, or the eraser end of pencil (with an unused eraser).

1. Use undiluted paint for thick dots or dilute paint with 50 percent water for smooth dots. Dip the tip into paint and then onto the surface. For uniform dots, redip in paint for each dot. For graduated dots, continue dotting with same paint load. Clean tip on paper towel after each group and reload.

Knob-and-Pole Printing

This is one of the simplest ways to create decorative printing for the beginner. Letters are made up of thin lines and dots. The letters can have a slight variation in size and still be pleasing to the eye. Always practice on paper first.

1. Print letters lightly on surface with pencil. Line the letters with desired paint color. Use undiluted paint for thick lines or thin paint with 50 percent water for thin lines.

2. Add a dot on each bend and ends of letters. For O, place dot on top, a bit to the left of center.

A Word About Glue

Glue can be a sticky subject when you don't use the right one. There are many glues on the market today, each formulated for a different crafting purpose.

White glue: This may be used as an all-purpose glue—it dries clear and flexible. It is often referred to as craft glue or tacky glue. Tacky on contact, it allows you to put two items together without a lot of set up time required. Use for most projects, especially ones involving wood, plastics, some fabrics, and cardboard.

Thin-bodied glues: Use these glues when your project requires a smooth, thin layer of glue. Thin-bodied glues work well on some fabrics and papers.

Fabric glue: This type of glue is made to bond with fabric fibers and withstand repeated washing. Use this kind of glue for attaching rhinestones and/or other charms to fabric projects. Some glues require heat-setting. Check the bottle for complete instructions.

Hot melt glue: Formed into cylindrical sticks, this glue is inserted into a hot temperature glue gun and heated to liquid state. Depending on the type of glue gun used, the glue is forced out through the gun's nozzle by either pushing on the end of the glue stick or squeezing a trigger. Use clear glue sticks for projects using wood, fabrics, most plastics, ceramics, and cardboard. When using any glue gun, be careful of the nozzle and the freshly applied glue—it is very hot! Apply glue to the piece being attached. Work with small areas at a time so that the glue doesn't set before being pressed into place.

Low melt glue: This is similar to hot melt glue in that it is formed into sticks and requires a glue gun to be used. Low melt glues are used for projects that would be damaged by heat. Examples include foam, balloons, and metallic ribbons. Low melt glue sticks are oval-shaped and can only be used in a low temperature glue gun.

Sewing

Before starting a sewing project, read through the directions and study the photographs to make sure you understand how the project is put together.

Materials

Fabrics: The type of fabric best suited to the project is given in the list of materials. But don't hesitate to make substitutions, taking into consideration your preferences in colors and patterns. Keep in mind the scale of a pattern relative to the size of the project. The weight of the fabric is an important consideration: Don't substitute a heavy, stiff fabric for a delicate fabric.

It is worth investing in the best materials you can afford. Many inexpensive fabrics are less likely to be colorfast. Avoid the regret that goes with choosing a fabric that isn't quite perfect but is less expensive than the fabric you really love.

Thread: Have mercerized sewing thread in the colors needed for the project you have chosen. Using the proper shade and strength (about a 50 weight) of thread avoids having the stitching show more than is necessary, and the item will have a finished look.

Fusible webbing (or adhesive): This lightweight fusible iron-on adhesive makes easy work of attaching fabric cutouts to your garment. The webbing is placed paper side up on the wrong side of the material. Place the iron on the paper side of the adhesive and press for one to three seconds. Allow the fabric to cool. Your design can then be drawn or traced onto the paper side and cut out. To transfer patterns to fusible webbing, place pattern piece right side down on the paper backing. Trace around the pattern piece and cut out. Remove the paper and place the material right side up in the desired position on your project and iron for three to five seconds. If desired, you may machine-stitch a zigzag stitch around the attached fusible adhesive pieces to secure the edges.

Tools

Scissors: For cutting fabric, you'll need sharp scissors eight to ten inches long with a bent handle. This style of scissors allows you to cut through the fabric while the fabric lies flat. These scissors should be used only for fabric. You'll also need a smaller pair of scissors, about six inches, with sharp points, for smaller projects and close areas.

Straight pins: Nonrusting dressmaker pins will not leave rust marks on your fabric if they come in contact with dampness or glue. And dressmaker's pins have very sharp points for easy insertion.

Ironing board and steam iron: The iron is just as important to a sewing project as the sewing machine. Keeping your fabrics, seams, and hems pressed saves valuable time and produces a professional look. You also use the iron to adhere fusible webbing. Be sure your ironing board is well padded and has a clean covering. Keep the bottom of your iron clean and free of any substance that could mark your fabric.

A steam-or-dry iron is best. The steam iron may be used directly on most fabrics with no shine. Test a small piece of the fabric first. If it causes a shine on the right side, try the reverse side.

Cutting Out Patterns

Some of the patterns in this book are smaller than actual size in order to fit them on the page. Instructions for enlarging patterns are on page 6. Many pattern pieces indicate that two pieces should be cut from the pattern. Fold the fabric in half, right sides together, lengthwise with the selvages together. Adjust one side to the left or right until the fabric hangs straight. The line created by the fold is parallel to the fabric's straight of grain. Place the pattern pieces right side up on the fabric with a straight arrow on the pattern lying along the grain line. A bent arrow indicates a line that should be placed on the fold. To make sure you have enough fabric, arrange and pin all pattern pieces on the fabric before you cut. Once the pieces are cut out, transfer any markings from the patterns to the fabric.

Stitching

Patterns include a seam allowance of ¼ inch, unless otherwise noted. The lettered dots on pattern pieces will help you fit pattern pieces together. A dot lettered A on one piece, for example, must be placed against the A dot on another piece. Pin fabric pieces right sides together before stitching.

Quilting

Material Selection

Fabric: The considerations for selecting fabrics for sewing projects apply to quilting as well. Try to select only 100 percent cotton fabrics for the face and back of the quilt. Cotton is easy to cut, mark, sew, and press. It is also widely available. Fabrics that contain synthetics, such as polyester, are more difficult to handle and are more likely to pucker.

The backing fabric should be similar in fiber content and care instructions to the fabrics used in the quilt top. Some wide cottons (90 and 108 inches) are sold specifically for quilt backings. They eliminate the need to piece the back.

Batting: Many types of batting are available to meet the needs of different projects. In general, use polyester batting with a low or medium loft. Polyester is better if the quilt will be washed frequently. All-cotton batting is preferred by some quilters for a very flat, traditional-looking quilt. For a puffier quilt, you can use a high-loft batting, but it is difficult to quilt.

Thread: Old, weak thread tangles and knots, making it frustrating to work with. Buy 100 percent cotton thread or good, long-staple polyester thread for piecing, appliqué, and machine quilting. Cotton quilting thread is wonderful for hand quilting, but should not be used for machine quilting because it is stiff and will tend to lie on the surface of the quilt.

For piecing by hand or by machine, select a neutral color of thread that blends in with most of the fabrics in the quilt. For most projects, either khaki or gray thread works well. Use white thread for basting; do not risk using colored thread, which could leave color behind. For appliqué, the thread should match the fabric that is being applied to the background. The color of quilting thread is a personal design choice. If you want your quilting to show up, use a contrasting color of thread.

Material Preparation

Prewashing: Always wash fabrics first. This will remove some of the chemicals added by the manufacturer, making it easier to quilt. Also, cotton fabric does shrink, and most of the shrinkage will occur during the first washing and drying. Be sure to use settings that are as hot as those you intend to use with the finished quilt.

Dark, intense colors, especially reds, tend to bleed or run. Wash these fabrics by themselves. If the water becomes colored, try soaking the fabric in a solution of three parts cold water to one part white wine vinegar. Rinse thoroughly. Wash again. If the fabric is still losing its color, discard the fabric and select another. It is not worth using a fabric that may ruin the other fabrics when the finished quilt is washed.

Marking and cutting fabric: Some of the patterns in this book are smaller than actual size in order to fit them on the page. Instructions for enlarging patterns are on page 6. To cut fabric the traditional way for piecing or ap-

pliqué, place the pattern right side down on the wrong side of the fabric. Trace around the pattern with a hard-lead pencil or a colored pencil designed for marking on fabric. Cut around each piece with sharp fabric scissors.

In many cases, it is faster and easier to cut fabric using a rotary cutter. This tool, which looks and works like a pizza cutter, must be used with a self-healing mat and a see-through ruler. Always use the safety shield of the rotary cutter when it is not in use.

Fold the fabric in half lengthwise with selvages together. Adjust one side until the fabric hangs straight. The line that is created by the fold is parallel to the fabric's straight of grain. Keeping this fold in place, lay the fabric on the mat. Place a see-through ruler on the fabric. Align one of the ruler's grid lines with the fold and trim the uneven edge of the fabric. Apply steady, even pressure to the rotary cutter and to the ruler to keep them and the fabric from shifting. Do not let the cutter get farther away from you than the hand that is holding the ruler. Stop cutting and reposition your hand.

Reposition the ruler so that it covers the width of the strip to be cut and the trimmed edge is on the markings for the appropriate measurement on the ruler.

After cutting the strip, hold it up to make sure it is straight. If it is angled, refold the fabric and trim it again. Continue cutting strips, checking frequently that the strips are straight.

Tools

A sharp pair of scissors is essential for cutting fabric. Keep another, separate pair of scissors for cutting out templates and other nonfabric uses.

To cut fabric quickly and easily, invest in a rotary cutter, see-through ruler, and self-healing mat. These tools let you cut strips of fabric efficiently.

The needles used for hand piecing and hand appliqué are called sharps. For hand quilting, use betweens (generally, start with a size 8 and work toward using a size 10 or 12). Use the smallest needle you can to make the smallest stitches.

Always use a sharp needle on your sewing machine; a dull needle will tend to skip stitches and snag the threads of your fabric, creating puckers.

Use fine, sharp straight pins (such as silk pins) for piecing and holding appliqué pieces in place before basting or stitching. Long quilter's pins are used to hold the three layers (top, batting, and backing) before they are basted together or quilted.

Piecing the Quilt

Unless otherwise noted, all seam allowances for projects in this book are ¼ inch. All projects in this book call for machine piecing. Hand piecing will work just as well, it will just take more of your time. When piecing, accuracy is important. A small error repeated in each block or, worse yet, in each seam, will become a large distortion. Before starting a large project, make a sample block and measure it. Is it the desired size? If not, figure out where the inaccuracy occurred. Are any seams a few threads too wide or narrow? Clip seams and restitch.

Machine piecing: When machine piecing, set the sewing machine's stitch length to 10 to 12 stitches per inch (or between 2 and 3 on machines that do not use the stitches per inch measure). Stitch across each seam allowance, along the seam line, and across the seam allowance at the far end of the seam. Do not backstitch.

Make sure the seam allowance is consistently ¼ inch.

Preparation for Quilting

Once you have made the blocks, sewn them together, and added borders according to the directions in the project, then it is time to quilt.

Decide what designs the quilting stitches will make. For a traditional look, outline important elements of the design with quilting. A grid of stitching works well in background areas. Fancier design elements that complement the theme of the quilt can also be incorporated. Make sure that there will be some stitching every few inches to secure the batting so that it does not shift.

Decide now if you need to mark the top for quilting. Simple outlining or grids can be marked as you quilt with masking tape. For more elaborate quilting designs, mark the top of the quilt. Use the lightest mark possible. Dark marks may be difficult to remove when the quilt is finished.

Spread out the backing (right side down) on a table or other flat surface. Use masking tape to secure it after smoothing it out. Place the batting on top of the backing, smoothing it out also. Finally, place the completed quilt top on the backing, right side up. Stretch it out so it is smooth and tape it.

For hand quilting, baste the layers together using long stitches. For best results, start basting at the center of the quilt and work toward the edges. Create a grid of basting by making a line of stitching approximately every four inches.

For machine quilting, baste by hand as described above

or use safety pins. Place a safety pin every three or four inches. To save time later, avoid placing pins on quilting lines.

Quilting

Quilting, stitching that goes through all three layers of the quilt, is both functional and decorative. It holds the batting in place. It is also an important design element, greatly enhancing the texture of the finished quilt.

To outline design areas, stitch ¼ inch away from each seam line. Simply decide where to stitch by eye or use ¼ inch masking tape placed along each seam as a guide. Masking tape can also be used as guides for straight lines and grids. Stitch beside the edge of the tape, avoiding stitching through the tape and getting the adhesive on the needle and thread. Do not leave the masking tape on the fabric when you are finished stitching each day, however, because it can leave a sticky residue that is difficult to remove.

Hand Quilting

Some quilters hold their work unsupported in their lap when they quilt. Most quilters, however, prefer to use some sort of quilting hoop or frame to hold the quilt stretched out. This makes it easier to stitch with an even tension and helps to prevent puckering and tucks.

Use betweens (quilting needles) for hand quilting. The smaller the needle (higher numbers like 11 and 12), the easier it will be to make small stitches. A quilting thimble on the third finger of your quilting hand will protect you from needle sores.

Use no more than 18 inches of quilting thread at once. Longer pieces of thread tend to tangle and the end gets worn as it is pulled through the fabric. Knot the end of the thread with a quilter's knot. Slip the needle into the quilt top and batting about an inch from where the first stitch should start. Pull the needle up through the quilt top at the beginning of the first stitch. Hold the thread

firmly and give it a little tug. The knot should pop into the batting and lodge between the quilt top and backing.

The quilting stitch is a running stitch. Place your free hand (left hand for right-handed people) under the quilt to feel for the needle as it pokes through. Load the needle with a couple of stitches by rocking the needle back and forth. At first, focus on making evenly sized stitches. Also, make sure you are going through all three layers. When you have mastered that, work on making the stitches smaller on future quilts.

Machine Quilting

Machine quilting is easy to learn, but it does take some practice. Make a few trial runs before starting to stitch on your completed quilt. On the test swatch, adjust the tension settings for the machine so that the stitches are even and do not pucker or have loose loops of thread.

The easiest machine stitching is long straight lines, starting at the center of the quilt and radiating out. These lines may be in a grid, stitched in the ditches formed by seams, outlines around design elements, or channels (long evenly spaced lines).

Whatever the pattern, quilt from the center to the outer edges. Plan the order of stitching before you begin. Your plan should minimize the need to start and stop.

Before placing the quilt on the sewing machine, roll the sides in toward the center and secure the rolls with pins or bicycle clips. Use an even-feed walking foot for straight lines of stitching. For freehand stitching, use a darning foot and lower the feed dogs or use a throat plate that covers the feed dogs.

To begin, turn the handwheel by hand to lower and raise the needle to its highest point. Pull gently on the top thread to bring the bobbin thread up through the quilt. Stitch in place for several stitches. Gradually increase the length of each stitch for the first ½ inch of quilting until the stitches are the desired length. This will secure the ends of the threads making it unnecessary to back-stitch or knot them. Reverse these steps at the end of each line of quilting.

When quilting with the even-feed walking foot, place your hands on either side of the presser foot and apply an even pressure. Keep the layers smooth and free of tucks.

Binding the Quilt

Binding may be made from strips of fabric that match or coordinate with the fabrics used in the quilt. These strips may be cut on the straight grain or on the bias. Straight binding is easier to cut and apply and can be used on most of the projects in this book. Quilts that have curved edges require bias binding. Also, bias bind-ing is stronger and tends to last longer. You can also purchase quilt binding. Apply according to the manufac-turer's instructions.

To make straight binding, cut strips of fabric 3¼ inches wide on the lengthwise or crosswise grain. For each side of the quilt, you will need a strip the length of that side plus two inches. For example, if the side measures 40 inches long, cut your strips 42 inches long.

Baste around the quilt, ¼ inch from the outer edge. Make sure all corners are square and trim any excess batting or fabric. Prepare each strip of binding by fold-ing it in half lengthwise, wrong sides together, and press. Find the center of each strip. Also find the center of each side of the quilt.

Place the binding strip on top of the quilt, aligning the raw edges of the strip and of the quilt and matching the centers. Stitch a ½-inch seam from one end of the quilt to the other. If you use an even-feed walking foot instead of the regular presser foot, it will be easier to keep the binding and the quilt smooth.

Trim the excess binding from each end. Fold the binding to the back of the quilt and slipstitch it in place. Repeat for the other opposite side of the quilt. Attach the binding to the ends of the quilt using the same procedure except do not trim the ends of the binding. Instead, fold the excess binding over the end of the quilt. Holding the end in place, fold the bind-ing to the back of the quilt and slipstitch in place.

Making a Hanging Sleeve

To make a sleeve for hanging a quilt, cut a strip of fabric (muslin or a scrap of backing fabric) six inches wide and as long as the quilt is wide. To finish the ends of the strip, roll under the ends to the wrong side of the fabric and slipstitch (or machine stitch). Fold the fabric lengthwise with wrong sides together. Stitch a ⅜-inch seam the length of the sleeve. Turn the sleeve wrong side out and press the seam. Stitch a ⅝-inch seam over the first seam. Turn the sleeve right side out and press. Stitch the sleeve to the top of the quilt and insert a dowel to hang the quilt.

WINTER

A WONDERLAND OF SNOW, ROSY CHEEKED CHILDREN SLEDDING DOWN HILLS, HOT CHOCOLATE WARMING COLD HANDS—EVEN THE HARDEST SEASON OFFERS SPECIAL DELIGHTS !

Starlight and Snoozing
Bear Can Covers

♥

M ake these adorable bears for a gift—the cans could hold delicious Caramel-Cinnamon Snack Mix, stationery, toiletries—they could even be small trash cans. Don't count on the bears to guard what's inside though, one's a real snoozer!

If we had no winter, the spring would not be so pleasant: if we did not sometimes taste of adversity, prosperity would not be so welcome.

Anne Bradstreet
Meditations Divine and Moral

2 large cans, about 7 inches tall × 6 inches in diameter

18 × 42-inch royal blue felt

10 × 14-inch dark heather brown plush felt

¼ yard hunter green plush felt

4 × 6-inch heather gray plush felt

8 × 11-inch gold felt

1⅓ yards fusible webbing

Scissors

Iron, ironing board

Press cloth (optional)

Black persian wool (or embroidery floss)

Embroidery needle with large eye

Tacky glue

STEP 2

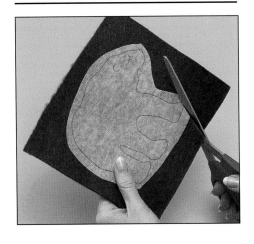

STEP 3

STEP 4

STEP 5

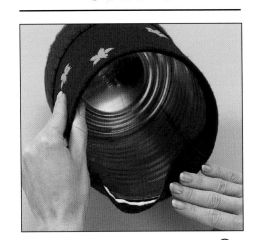

Enlarge pattern 135%.

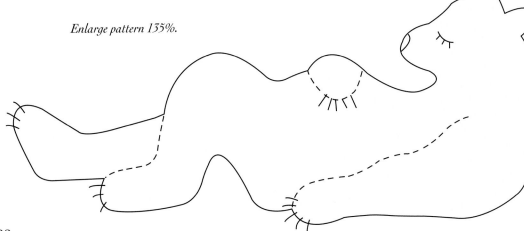

1 Remove label, wash can, and check top for sharp edges. (Hint: Use label to determine size to cut background.) Cut background royal blue felt 1 inch taller and ½ inch longer than can.

2 Trace bears, ground patterns, tree trunk, tree top, and 16 stars onto paper side of fusible webbing. (Ground patterns are repeated around can.) Fuse bears to dark heather brown, ground patterns and tree top to hunter green, tree trunk to heather gray, and stars to gold felt. (Hint: Test felt scrap with iron before fusing. If iron drags, use a press cloth and steam to set fusible webbing.) Cut out all appliqués.

3 Referring to photos, fuse appliqués to background.

4 Using 1 strand of persian wool, work a buttonhole stitch across top edge of ground and around tree. Use short straight stitches to suggest buttonhole stitch around the stars. For bears, embroider noses with wool. Outline eyelashes, ears, and claws with long straight stitches. For snoozing bear, sew a straight stitch as shown by dotted lines on pattern to define bear's arms and legs.

5 Glue appliquéd background to can, overlapping where ends join and leaving 1 inch above can top. Fold and glue 1 inch over top edge and into can. (Hint: Use clothespins to hold until glue sets.)

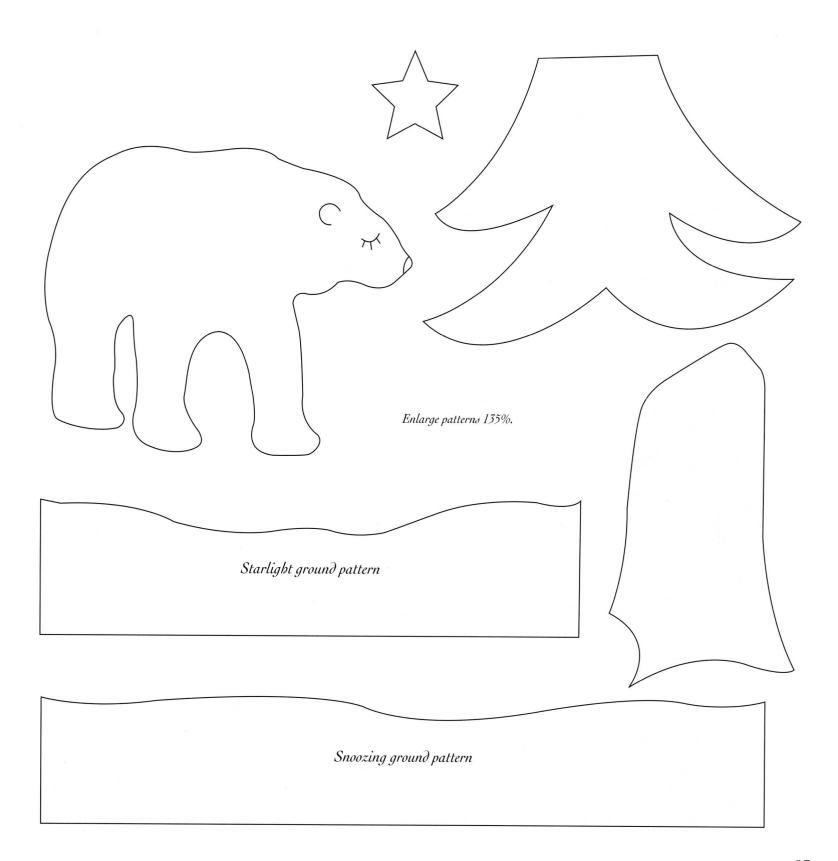

Enlarge patterns 135%.

Starlight ground pattern

Snoozing ground pattern

23

Caramel-Cinnamon Snack Mix

♥

2 tablespoons vegetable oil
½ cup popcorn kernels
½ teaspoon salt, divided
1½ cups packed light brown sugar
½ cup butter or margarine
½ cup corn syrup
¼ cup red-hot cinnamon candies
2 cups cinnamon-flavored bear-
    shaped graham crackers
1 cup red and green candy-
    coated chocolate pieces

1 Grease 2 large baking pans. Set aside.

2 Heat oil in large saucepan over high heat until hot. Add corn kernels. Cover pan. Shake pan constantly over heat until kernels no longer pop.

3 Divide popcorn evenly between 2 large bowls. Add ¼ teaspoon salt to each bowl; toss to coat. Set aside.

4 Preheat oven to 250°F. Combine sugar, butter, and corn syrup in heavy, medium saucepan. Cook over medium heat until sugar melts, stirring constantly with wooden spoon. Bring mixture to a boil. Boil 5 minutes, stirring frequently.

5 Remove ½ of sugar mixture (about ¾ cup) from saucepan; pour over 1 portion of popcorn. Toss with lightly greased spatula until evenly coated.

6 Add red-hot candies to saucepan. Stir constantly with wooden spoon until melted. Pour over remaining portion of popcorn; toss with lightly greased spatula until evenly coated.

7 Spread each portion of popcorn in even layer in separate prepared pans with lightly greased spatula.

8 Bake 1 hour, stirring every 15 minutes with wooden spoon to prevent popcorn from sticking together.

9 Cool completely in pans. Combine popcorn, graham crackers, and chocolate pieces in large bowl.

10 Store in airtight container at room temperature up to 1 week.

Makes about 4 quarts

Spiced Red Wine

♥

The Grape Ice Ring adds a special touch to this traditional holiday punch. ♥

Grape Ice Ring (recipe follows)
½ cup sugar
½ cup water
1 bottle Burgundy wine, chilled
2 cups white grape juice, chilled
1 cup peach schnapps, chilled

1 Prepare Grape Ice Ring.

2 Combine sugar and water in a small saucepan. Bring to a boil. Boil, stirring constantly, until sugar is dissolved. Cool to room temperature. Cover; refrigerate until chilled, about 2 hours.

3 Combine wine, grape juice, schnapps, and sugar syrup in punch bowl. Float Grape Ice Ring in punch.

Makes 14 servings (about 4 ounces each)

GRAPE ICE RING
2 pounds assorted seedless grapes
    (Thompson, Red Empress, etc.)
Lemon leaves,* optional

Fill 4-cup ring mold with water to within ¾ inch of top. Freeze until firm, about 8 hours or overnight. Arrange clusters of grapes and leaves on ice as shown in photo; fill with water to top of mold. Freeze until solid. To unmold, dip bottom of mold briefly in hot water.
*These nontoxic leaves are available in florist shops.

Happy Holiday Vest

♥

If you've been looking for that special outfit to wear to a holiday party, why not make it yourself? This vest can be made in one day for a weekend gathering. No one will believe how easy it is to make!♥

WHAT YOU'LL NEED

1½ × 22-inch strip each red and gold print fabrics

9 × 14-inches each green print and off-white print fabrics

14 × 15½-inch beige print

10 × 11-inch green print

9 × 14-inch gold print

14 × 14½-inch blue print

½ yard fusible webbing

Appliqué fabrics: 8 × 8-inch white on white, 7 × 7-inch red print, 4 × 4-inch red print, 7 × 7-inch green print, 2 × 2-inch brown solid, 2 × 2-inch yellow print, 2 × 2-inch black, 4 × 4-inch gold print, 3 × 3-inch brown print

Thread: white, black, brown, yellow, dark gold

1½ yards lining and back fabric

Your favorite vest pattern

7 black seed beads

3 buttons, ¾ inch each

6 buttons, various colors and sizes

STEP 1

STEP 2

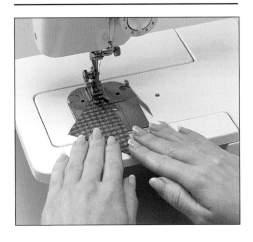

STEP 4

STEP 5

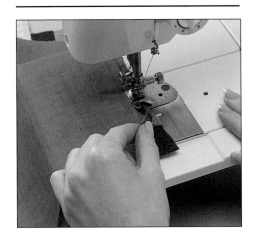

1 To make checked piece: Stitch 1½-inch strip red print to 1½-inch strip gold print along 22-inch length. Cut into 1½-inch-wide sections. Cut 14 sections. Stitch sections together, alternating colors to form checked piece.

2 To make pinwheel section: Cut 14 triangles (see pattern) each of green print and off-white print fabric (dashed line is stiching line).

Stitch a green triangle to an off-white triangle on the diagonal side to form a square. Repeat for all triangles.

3 Stitch 4 squares together to create a pinwheel. Stitch pinwheel blocks together to make a row.

4 To make vest front: Stitch checked piece to top of 14 × 15½-inch beige print.

STEP 6

STEP 9

STEP 8

STEP 12

9 Peel off paper back from all pieces and press on vest fronts, following finished photo.

10 Using blanket stitch on sewing machine, appliqué all pieces on vest fronts. Use thread colors as follows: black for tree, mitten, hat, house; white for mitten cuff, snowman, snow; yellow for window; brown for door, trunk; and gold for star, scarf. Knot all threads on back of fabric.

11 Cut out remaining vest pieces and assemble vest following pattern directions.

12 Stitch beads to snowman for eyes, nose, and mouth. Stitch buttons to snowman, star, and door at Xs.

5 Stitch 10 × 11-inch green print to top of checked piece, lining up pieces along right edge. Cut out right front of vest.

6 To make left front: Stitch pinwheel section to top of 9 × 14-inch gold print.

7 Stitch 14 × 14½-inch blue print to top of pinwheel section, lining up pieces along left edge. Cut out left front of vest.

8 To make appliqués: Following manufacturer's directions, iron fusible webbing to back of all appliqué fabrics. Trace appliqué patterns onto the paper and cut out all pieces.

Enlarge patterns 150%.

Country Pecan Pie

Pie pastry for single 9-inch
   pie crust
1¼ cups dark corn syrup
  4 eggs
  ½ cup packed light brown sugar
  ¼ cup butter or margarine,
   melted
  2 teaspoons all-purpose flour
1½ teaspoons vanilla extract
1½ cups pecan halves

1 Preheat oven to 350°F. Roll pastry on lightly floured surface to form 13-inch circle. Fit into 9-inch pie plate. Trim edges; flute. Set aside.

2 Combine corn syrup, eggs, brown sugar, and melted butter in large bowl; beat with electric mixer on medium speed until well blended.

3 Stir in flour and vanilla until blended. Pour into unbaked pie crust. Arrange pecans on top.

4 Bake 40 to 45 minutes until center of filling is puffed and golden brown. Cool completely on wire rack. Garnish as desired.

Makes one 9-inch pie

This rich, delicious pie will have your guests wanting seconds! ♥

Oyster Corn Stew

♥

Nothing is better than warm stew on a cold, blustery day! Your family will enjoy this delicious treat. ♥

40 medium oysters or 1 pint
    shucked fresh oysters
    including liquor*
  Salt
1 cup milk
1 can (15 ounces) cream-style
    corn
¼ teaspoon salt
¼ teaspoon celery seeds
  Dash ground white pepper
4 tablespoons butter or
    margarine
1 rib celery, chopped
1 cup cream or half-and-half
  Celery leaves and lemon zest
    for garnish

1 Scrub oysters thoroughly with stiff brush under cold running water. Soak oysters in mixture of ⅓ cup salt to 1 gallon water for 20 minutes. Drain water; repeat 2 more times.

2 Place on tray and refrigerate 1 hour to help oysters relax. To shuck oysters, take pointed oyster knife in 1 hand and thick towel or glove in the other. With towel, grip shell in palm of hand. Keeping oyster level with knife, insert tip of knife between the shell next to hinge; twist to pry shell until you hear a snap. (Use knife as leverage; do not force.)

3 Twist to open shell, keeping oyster level at all times to save liquor. Cut the muscle from shell and discard top shell. Tip shell over strainer in bowl to catch oysters; discard bottom shell. Refrigerate oysters. Strain oyster liquor from bowl through triple thickness of dampened cheesecloth into small bowl; set aside oyster liquor.

4 Place milk, corn, ¼ teaspoon salt, celery seeds, and pepper in large saucepan. Bring to a simmer over medium heat; set aside.

5 Melt butter in medium skillet over medium-high heat. Add celery and cook 8 to 10 minutes or until tender. Add reserved oyster liquor; cook until heated through. Add oysters; heat about 10 minutes, just until oysters begin to curl around edges.

6 Add oyster mixture and cream to milk mixture. Cook over medium-high heat until just heated through. Do not boil.

7 Serve in wide-rimmed soup bowls. Garnish, if desired.

Makes 6 servings

*Liquor is the term used to describe the natural juices of an oyster.

Country Folk Santa

This folk art Santa is sure to fly into your heart and become part of your family holiday traditions. If you don't have a jigsaw, you can have your local lumber store cut out the shapes for you. This Santa is worth the effort!♥

WHAT YOU'LL NEED

1-inch pine board

Stylus

Graphite paper

Jigsaw

Sandpaper

Tack cloth

Drill, small drill bit

Waterbase varnish

Acrylic paint: buttermilk, ebony black, country red, green meadow

Brushes: small flat, 10/0 liner

Jute twine

Announced by all the trumpets of the sky,
Arrives the snow.

Ralph Waldo Emerson
"The Snowstorm"

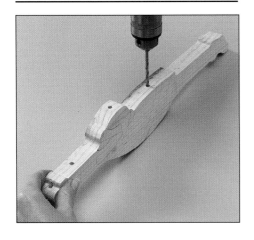

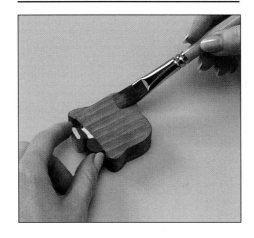

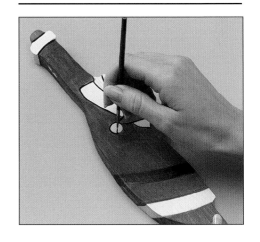

1 Apply pattern to wood using stylus and graphite paper.

2 Cut out Santa and bag from wood. Sand until smooth and use tack cloth to remove dust. Drill 2 holes through the thickness of the wood: 1 in top of hands and second approximately 1½ inches closer to the head. Make sure holes are completely through. Drill holes through bag also, the same distance apart as holes in arms. Drill 2 shallow holes on the top edge of Santa (about ¼ inch deep).

3 Mix varnish and acrylic paint to make a stain. Test on sample wood for proper transparency. Wrap color around edge (thickness) of wood. Leave Santa's face bare. Fur, beard, and candy cane are buttermilk. Belt and boots are ebony black. Suit, ball, and candy stripe are country red. Gloves and bag are green meadow. Let dry.

4 Line entire pattern with ebony black.

5 Splatter front and thicknesses of wood with ebony black.

6 Finish entirely with varnish.

7 Cut two 4-inch pieces of jute twine. Tie a knot in 1 end of twine. Thread from bottom of bag through drilled hole. Continue with same piece adding the arm and tie a knot in the end. This will hold the bag in place. Take second piece of twine and repeat. For the hanger, cut a 12-inch piece of twine. Tie a tight bow in the center of the twine. Insert glue in shallow drilled holes and push twine ends in holes and let dry.

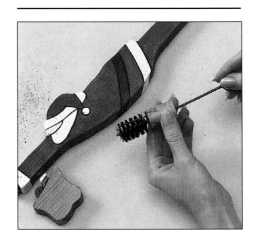

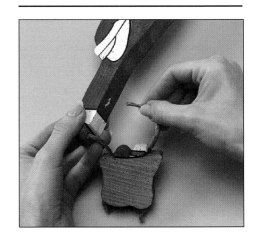

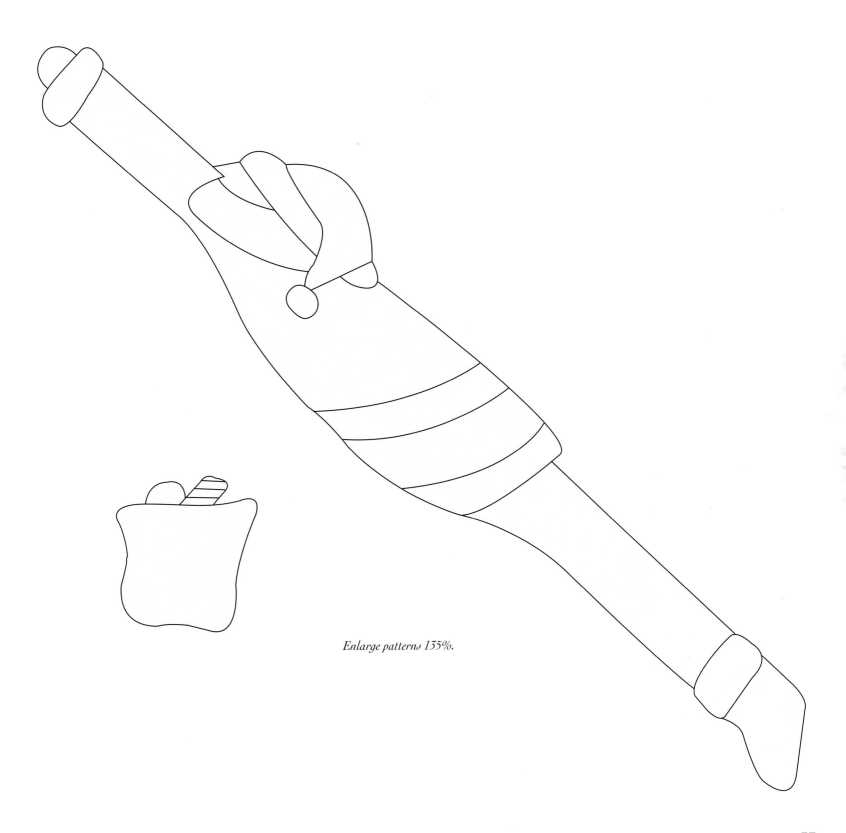

Enlarge patterns 135%.

Gingerbread Folks

♥

Give ordinary gingerbread people more personality by bending their arms and legs into dancing poses before you pop them in the oven! ♥

½ cup shortening
⅓ cup packed light brown sugar
¼ cup dark molasses
1 egg white
⅓ teaspoon vanilla
1½ cups all-purpose flour
½ teaspoon baking soda
¼ teaspoon baking powder
½ teaspoon salt
1 teaspoon ground cinnamon
½ teaspoon ground ginger
Assorted food colors
Vanilla frosting and assorted
    decorating gels
Assorted candies and
    decorations
6-inch gingerbread boy and
    girl cookie cutters

1. Beat shortening, brown sugar, molasses, egg white, and vanilla in large bowl at high speed of electric mixer until smooth. Combine flour, baking soda, baking powder, salt, and spices in small bowl. Add to shortening mixture; mix well. Cover; refrigerate until firm, about 8 hours or overnight.

2. Preheat oven to 350°F. Grease cookie sheets.

3. Roll dough on floured surface to ⅛-inch thickness. Cut out cookies with cookie cutters. Place on prepared cookie sheets. Bend arms and legs to make cookies look like they're dancing.

4. Bake 8 to 10 minutes or until edges begin to brown. Remove to wire racks; cool completely.

5. Color frosting as desired. Decorate as shown in photo.

Makes about 6 large cookies

Lollipop Cookies

♥

A whimsical treat is formed by sandwiching a luscious chocolate filling between two butter cookies. ♥

1½ cup butter or margarine, softened
½ cup granulated sugar
½ cup packed light brown sugar
2 egg yolks
3½ cups all-purpose flour
1½ teaspoon baking powder
¼ teaspoon salt
1 cup semisweet chocolate chips, melted
½ cup finely chopped hazelnuts or almonds
1 cup vanilla frosting (about ½ of 16 oz. container)
Red and green decorating gel
Colored sugars
2-inch round cookie cutter
24 (4-inch) lollipop sticks*

1 Combine butter, granulated sugar, brown sugar, and egg yolks in medium bowl. Add flour, baking powder, and salt; mix well. Cover; refrigerate until firm, about 4 hours or overnight.

2 Preheat oven to 350°F. Grease cookie sheets.

3 Roll dough on floured surface to ¼-inch thickness. Cut out 48 circles using cookie cutter. Place 24 circles on prepared cookie sheets.

4 Combine melted chocolate and hazelnuts. Spoon rounded ½ teaspoon chocolate mixture in center of each dough circle on cookie sheet. Place lollipop sticks on circles so that tips of sticks are embedded in filling. Top with remaining dough circles; seal edges of dough together with floured fork tines.

5 Bake 10 to 12 minutes until edges begin to brown. Remove to wire racks; cool completely.

6 Frost tops and sides of cookies with vanilla frosting. Decorate with decorating gel and colored sugars as shown in photo.

Makes 2 dozen sandwich cookies
*Lollipop sticks are available at stores carrying cake decorating supplies.

40

Chocolate Snowflakes

♥

Paper snowflakes — the kind you used to make as a child — act as stencils to create snowy sugar patterns atop these yummy cookies. ♥

1 cup butter or margarine,
    softened
1 cup sugar
1 egg
1 teaspoon vanilla
2 ounces semisweet chocolate,
    melted
2¼ cups all-purpose flour
1 teaspoon baking powder
¼ teaspoon salt
    3-inch round cookie cutter
    Parchment paper
    Confectioners' sugar

1 Beat butter and sugar in large bowl at high speed of electric mixer until fluffy. Beat in egg and vanilla. Add melted chocolate; mix well. Add flour, baking powder, and salt; mix well. Cover; refrigerate until firm, about 2 hours.

2 Preheat oven to 325°F. Grease cookie sheets.

3 Roll dough on floured surface to ⅛-inch thickness. Using 3-inch cookie cutter, cut into circles. Place 1 inch apart on prepared cookie sheets.

4 Bake 8 to 10 minutes until edges begin to brown. Remove to wire racks; cool completely.

5 To make snowflakes, cut several pieces of parchment paper into 3-inch circles. Fold each in half, then into quarters. With scissors, cut small pieces from folded edges to create snowflake design.

6 Unfold circles and place on top of cooled cookies. Sift confectioners' sugar generously over paper patterns. Carefully remove paper. Repeat with remaining cookies.

Makes about 2 dozen cookies

Cranberry Cedar Wreath

WHAT YOU'LL NEED

15-inch birch wreath

Wire cutters

5 stems preserved cedar

3 stems preserved fir

Hot glue gun, glue sticks

22-gauge floral wire

4 to 5 pinecones

4 to 5 stems silk red cranberries, each with 2 bunches of berries and 1 bud

1 yard red and green cloth Christmas ribbon

Convey a warm welcome with this fragrant holiday wreath. ♥

1 Cut cedar and fir 10 to 18 inches long and hot glue in a circular motion around wreath following the lines of extending branches.

2 Cut a long length of wire and wrap wire around bottom of pinecones. Randomly attach cones to wreath.

3 Cut cranberry stems 10 to 15 inches long and hot glue in a circular motion around the center of the wreath.

4 Make a 2-loop bow and attach to wreath with floral wire on the center of right side.

Even the seasons form a great circle in their changing, and always come back again to where they were.

Black Elk
"Black Elk Speaks, Being the Life..."

43

Gingerbread House

♥

5¼ cups all-purpose flour
  1 tablespoon ginger
  2 teaspoons baking soda
1½ teaspoons allspice
  1 teaspoon salt
  2 cups packed dark brown sugar
  1 cup plus 2 tablespoons butter
    or margarine, softened
  ¾ cup dark corn syrup
  2 large eggs
    Royal Icing (recipe follows)
    Assorted gum drops, hard
     candies, and decors

1 Draw patterns for house on cardboard, using diagrams on this page as guides; cut out patterns. Preheat oven to 375°F. Grease large cookie sheet.

2 Place flour, ginger, baking soda, allspice, and salt in medium bowl; stir to combine.

3 Beat brown sugar and butter in large bowl with electric mixer at medium speed until light and fluffy, scraping down side of bowl once. Beat in corn syrup and eggs. Gradually add flour mixture. Beat at low speed until well blended, scraping down side of bowl once.

4 Roll about ¼ of dough directly onto prepared cookie sheet to ¼-inch thickness. Lay sheet of waxed paper over dough. Place patterns over waxed paper 2 inches apart. Cut dough around patterns with sharp knife; remove waxed paper. Reserve scraps to reroll with next batch of dough.

5 Bake 15 minutes or until no indentation remains when cookie is touched in center. While cookies are still hot, place cardboard pattern lightly over cookie; trim edges with sharp knife to straighten. Let stand on cookie sheet 5 minutes. Remove cookies with spatula to wire racks; cool completely. Repeat with remaining pattern pieces.

6 Prepare Royal Icing. Some Icing may be divided into small bowls and tinted with food coloring to use for decorative piping.

7 Cover 12-inch square piece of heavy cardboard with aluminum foil to use as base for house.

8 Place Icing in small resealable plastic freezer bag. Cut off small corner of bag. Pipe Icing on edges of all pieces including bottom; "glue" house together at seams and onto base. Pipe door, shutters, etc. onto front of house. Decorate as desired with Icing and candies. If desired, dust house with sifted powdered sugar to resemble snow.

Makes 1 gingerbread house

ROYAL ICING
  1 egg white,* at room
    temperature
  2 to 2½ cups sifted powdered
    sugar
  ½ teaspoon almond extract

Beat egg white in small bowl with electric mixer at high speed until foamy. Gradually add 2 cups powdered sugar and almond extract. Beat at low speed until moistened. Increase mixer speed to high and beat until Icing is stiff.
*Use only grade A clean, uncracked eggs.

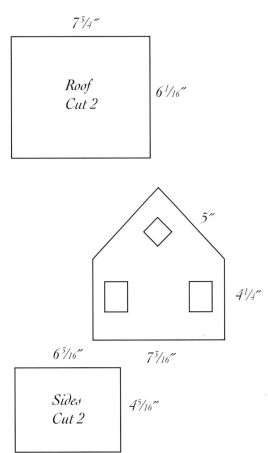

44

Fuzzie Bear

This adorable bear will add warmth to any room of your house. ♥

WHAT YOU'LL NEED

20 × 45-inch piece cotton batting

1 package tan dye

White paper, pencil

Pins

Scissors

Thread, needle

10 yards brown bedspread cotton or pearl cotton, size 5

10 ounces polyester fiberfill

1 yard brown embroidery floss

2 × 36-inch blue print for ribbon

2 black buttons, ⅜ inch each

I hear America singing, the varied carols I hear.

Walt Whitman
"I Hear America Singing"

STEP 4

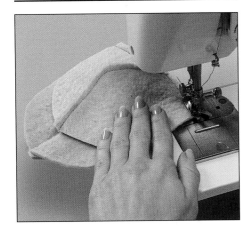

STEP 5

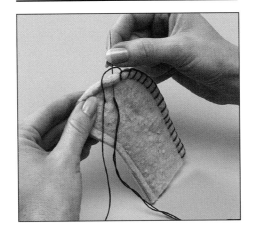

STEP 6

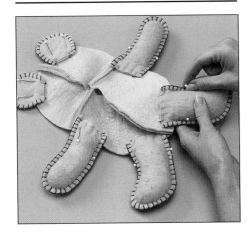

STEP 8

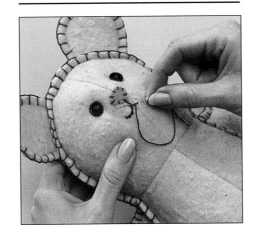

1 Following manufacturer's directions, wash and dry batting. Following manufacturer's directions, dye batting tan in sink.

2 Trace all pattern pieces on paper. Fold batting in half, right sides together. Pin and cut out all pattern pieces on 2 layers of batting. (Note: All seam allowances are ½ inch.)

3 With right sides together, stitch head front seam, head back seam, body front seam, and body back seam. Clip curves.

4 With right sides together, stitch front head to front body at neck. Stitch back head to back body at neck, leaving open space to stuff where marked.

5 All remaining seams are stitched wrong side to wrong side, so seams will be exposed. Stitch legs, arms, and ears, leaving open to stuff where marked. Using brown cotton, blanket stitch around seamed edges. Stuff legs and arms to 1 inch below top. Baste openings closed.

6 Pin legs, arms, and ears to wrong side of back head and body section. Place front head and body section on back section, wrong sides together. Pin in place and stitch around head and body sections.

7 Stuff head and body section and stitch opening closed. Blanket stitch around head and body.

8 Using brown embroidery floss, stitch on eyes, nose, and mouth.

9 Fold 2½ × 36-inch blue fabric in half to measure 1¼ × 36 inches. Stitch ends and sides, leaving an opening in the middle to turn. Turn and stitch opening closed. Tie in a bow at the neck of the bear.

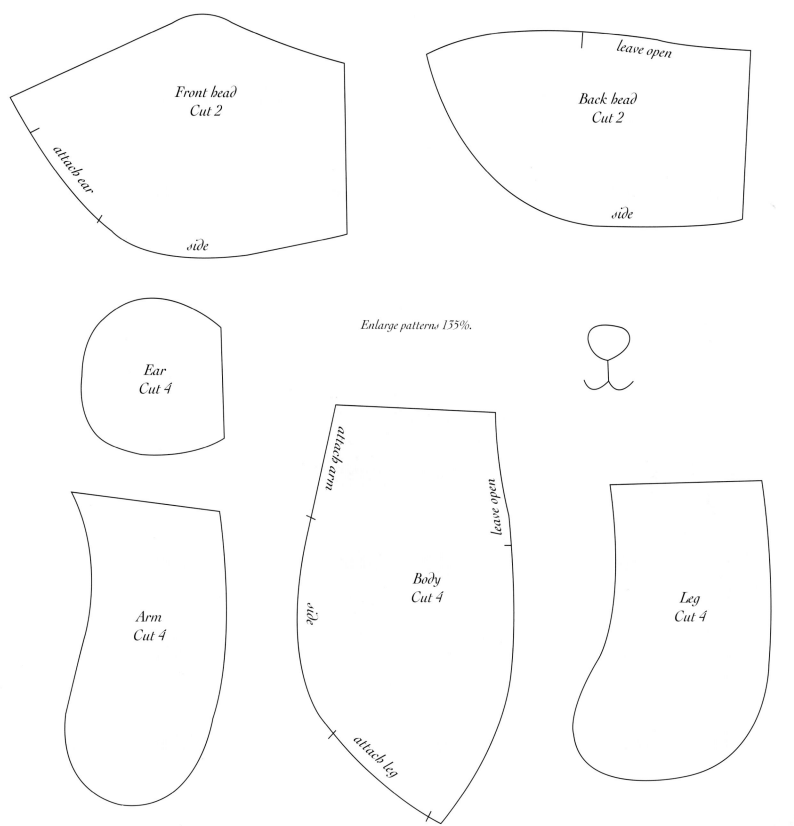

Front head
Cut 2

attach ear

side

Back head
Cut 2

leave open

side

Ear
Cut 4

Enlarge patterns 135%.

Arm
Cut 4

attach arm

side

Body
Cut 4

leave open

attach leg

Leg
Cut 4

Winter Wonderland Birdhouse

WHAT YOU'LL NEED

3 pieces wood ($2 \times 4 \times 3\frac{1}{2}$ inches, $1 \times 12 \times 11\frac{1}{2}$ inches, $1 \times 4 \times 3\frac{1}{2}$ inches)

Hand saw

Sandpaper

Tack cloth

Drill, 1-inch wood drill bit

Large cloud birdhouse

1-inch wood dowel, 3 feet long

Acrylic paint: burnt umber, snow white, country red

1-inch brush

Crackle medium

Wood glue

Matte finishing spray

Pine garland

Hot glue gun, glue sticks

Silk holly branches

Decorative cardinal

T his birdhouse will bring you a touch of winter charm. ♥

STEP 2

STEP 3

4 Glue 1-inch support to the center of the bottom of the birdhouse with wood glue. Glue 2-inch support to the center of the base and let dry. Line up the house and the base so they are both square. Glue pole to base and to house.

5 Spray entirely with matte finishing spray and let dry.

6 Garnish with pine garland. Begin at bottom base and attach end to base with hot glue. Twist garland up and around pole, gluing on back side of pole. Continue over side of house and drape over roof and around front corner of house.

STEP 6

STEP 7

7 Add sprigs of holly with berries in 3 separate groupings on pole, and 1 grouping on center peak of roof. Attach cardinal on top of house.

1 Cut wood to appropriate sizes, sand rough edges, and tack off excess dust. Drill a hole through middle of the 2 small blocks (pole supports) of wood. Basecoat entire birdhouse and bottom base (large wood piece) with burnt umber. Basecoat pole (dowel) with snow white. Basecoat pole supports with country red. Let all pieces dry.

2 Apply crackle medium (following manufacturer's directions) on entire birdhouse and bottom base. Let dry completely.

3 Paint birdhouse walls with snow white. Paint roof, eaves, bottom of birdhouse, perch, and base with country red. Wait until white paint is finished cracking and is dry before painting red.

Country Christmas Blocks

♥

These decorative Christmas blocks make a great centerpiece on any holiday table. When on the table with Spicy Corn Muffins and Meaty Chili, these blocks are the perfect decorative accent to a hot and hearty meal. ♥

WHAT YOU'LL NEED

3 wood blocks, 4 × 4 inches each

Sandpaper

Tack cloth

Oak gel stain

Wood sealer

White graphite

Stylus

Acrylic paint: burnt umber, buttermilk, country red, ebony black, pumpkin, flesh tone, evergreen

Brushes: #2 flat, ½-inch flat, 10/0 liner

Waterbase varnish

STEP 1

STEP 2

STEP 5

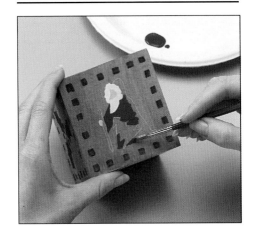

STEP 6

1 Slightly sand all edges of wood blocks and tack off excess dust. Stain the smooth sides of all blocks with oak stain. The rough-cut sides absorb stain faster, so use 1 part oak stain and 1 part wood sealer on them. Let dry.

2 Center and apply patterns with white graphite and stylus.

3 Base the following colors in designated areas (let each color dry before applying the next): snowman, Santa's beard and fur, and candy cane with buttermilk; Santa's face and hand with flesh tone; holly leaves with evergreen; berries with country red. Square trim around top of block is alternating colors of evergreen and country red. Square trim around

sides of block is all country red. Square trim around candy cane, snowman, and Santa is evergreen.

4 Apply detail pattern with graphite where needed.

5 Apply remaining colors in designated areas: snowman's scarf, Santa's coat, and stripes on candy cane are based with country red. Base carrot with pumpkin. The tree is based with evergreen. Tree branch and Santa's cane are based with burnt umber.

6 Base snowman's hat and line all patterns with ebony black.

7 After all blocks are finished and completely dry, wash entire block with wash of waterbase varnish and diluted burnt umber. Caution: This should be transparent and merely to age painting. Test on paper for transparency— you can always let it dry and repeat for more color.

8 Splatter fronts of blocks with ebony black.

55

Spicy Corn Muffins

1 cup low fat buttermilk
1 tablespoon vegetable oil
1 egg white
1 serrano pepper, minced
1 cup cornmeal
⅓ cup all-purpose flour
1 tablespoon finely chopped
    fresh cilantro or parsley
1 teaspoon baking powder
½ teaspoon baking soda
¼ teaspoon salt
¼ teaspoon ground cumin
¼ teaspoon ground paprika

1 Preheat oven to 400°F. Spray 6-cup muffin pan with nonstick cooking spray.

2 Combine buttermilk, oil, egg white, and serrano pepper in small bowl until smooth.

3 Combine cornmeal, flour, cilantro, baking powder, baking soda, salt, cumin, and paprika in medium bowl; mix well. Make well in center of dry ingredients; pour in buttermilk mixture. Stir with fork just until dry ingredients are moistened.

4 Spoon batter evenly into muffin cups. Bake 15 to 20 minutes or until toothpick inserted in center comes out clean.

Makes 6 muffins

Meaty Chili

1 large onion
2 fresh jalapeño peppers
2 cloves garlic, minced
1 pound coarsely ground beef for chili
¼ pound ground Italian sausage
2 medium ribs celery, diced
1 can (28 ounces) tomatoes, cut-up, undrained
1 can (15 ounces) pinto beans, drained
1 can (12 ounces) tomato juice (1½ cups)
1 cup water
¼ cup ketchup
1 teaspoon sugar
1 teaspoon chili powder
½ teaspoon salt
½ teaspoon ground cumin
½ teaspoon dried thyme leaves, crushed
⅛ teaspoon ground black pepper
    Red bell pepper and fresh herb sprig for garnish

1 To chop onion, peel skin. Cut onion in half through root with utility knife. Place cut side down on cutting board. Cut onion into thin slices perpendicular to root end, holding onion with fingers to keep its shape; then turn onion and cut crosswise to root end. Repeat with remaining onion half.

2 To chop jalapeño peppers,* cut each pepper in half lengthwise, remove seeds, cut into strips, then chop. Wash your hands after handling the chili peppers.

3 Cook onion, jalapeño peppers, garlic, beef, sausage, and celery in a 5-quart Dutch oven over medium-high heat until meat loses its red color and onion is tender, stirring frequently to break up meat.

4 Stir in tomatoes, beans, tomato juice, water, ketchup, sugar, chili powder, salt, cumin, thyme, and black pepper. Bring to a boil over high heat. Reduce heat to medium-low; simmer, uncovered, 30 minutes, stirring occasionally.

5 Ladle into bowls. Garnish, if desired.

Makes 6 servings
*Chili peppers can sting and irritate the skin; wear rubber gloves when handling peppers and do not touch eyes. Wash your hands after handling chili peppers.

Amber Lee

♥

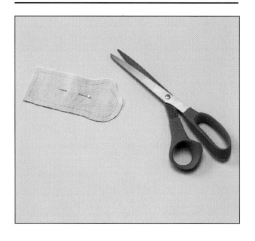

This delightfully versatile country doll can be decorated to represent any special occasion. ♥

WHAT YOU'LL NEED

¼ yard unbleached muslin

1 package tan dye

6 ounces polyester fiberfill

2 × 14-inch piece black fabric

5 × 14-inch piece red and tan stripe

1 ounce brown yarn, 4 ply

1 yard blue ribbon, ⅛ inch wide

Felt-tip fabric markers: black, red

Blusher

½ yard blue plaid

4½ × 10-inch piece osnaburg cloth

4-inch square fusible webbing

2-inch square each red, blue, and green print

2 yards black embroidery floss

1 each ⁷⁄₁₆-inch burgundy, red, white, and 2 blue buttons

4 round hook-and-loop fasteners, ½ inch each

4 × 8-inch piece red plaid

8-inch square cotton batting

3-inch square yellow print

2 × 8-inch blue print

3 × 8-inch piece red and white stripe

1 Wash and dry unbleached muslin. Do not use fabric softener. Following manufacturer's directions, dye the unbleached muslin tan.

2 Trace and cut out all doll pattern pieces. Leg-shoe is cut as one piece and seam line is marked.

3 With muslin folded (9 × 22 inches), trace arm twice and head-body, leaving at least ½ inch of space between pieces. Traced lines are seam lines. Cut around all pieces ¼ inch away from seam lines.

4 Stitch around arms, leaving open at top. Clip curves and turn arms right side out. Lightly stuff hand area with fiberfill. Stitch lines for fingers. Stuff arms to 1 inch below top. Baste top closed.

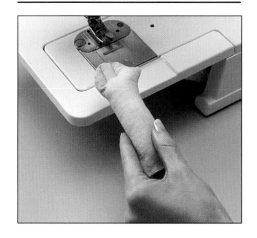

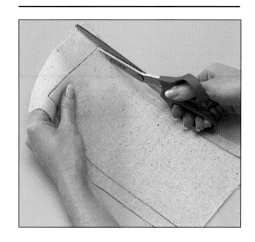

8 Stitch legs to front body at opening, making sure feet are forward. Stuff head and body and stitch opening closed.

9 Cut yarn into 14-inch lengths. Stitch center of each hair to head at seam line. Stitch hair to front and back of head along stitching lines. Cut ribbon in half and tie hair into ponytails. Trim hair.

5 Stitch from A to B around head. Pin arms in place at sides. Stitch sides catching arms in seams. Clip curves and turn right side out.

6 Stitch 2 × 14-inch black fabric to 5 × 14-inch red and tan stripe fabric. Press seam to the black fabric. Fold fabric in half, right sides together. On wrong side of fabric trace leg-shoe twice, lin-

ing up seam line on pattern to seam of fabric (leave at least ½ inch between pieces). Cut out leg-shoe ¼ inch from traced lines.

7 Stitch around leg-shoe on traced lines, leaving top open. Clip curves and turn right side out. Stuff to 1 inch below top. Place seams together and baste across top.

10 Paint eyes and mouth on face with fabric markers. Using finger, put blusher on cheeks.

11 To make dress: Cut dress bodice front and back and skirt (5½ × 20 inches) from blue plaid. Cut apron (4½ × 10 inches) from osnaburg cloth.

12 Stitch dress bodice front and back at sleeves and sides.

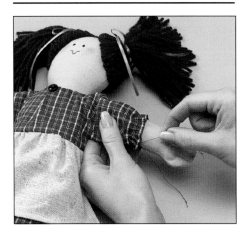

16 Put dress on doll. Stitch dress closed at neck back and stitch blue button over stitches. Take a tuck at center of neck front and stitch burgundy button at tuck. Stitch a running stitch around sleeves and gather sleeves around arms.

17 Stitch ½-inch round hook end of hook-and-loop tape to right hand.

18 To make heart: Cut 2 red plaid hearts. Cut out 1 batting heart. Layer fabric hearts, right sides out, with batting between. Using black embroidery floss, stitch around outside with a running stitch, through all layers.

19 Cut out yellow for yoyo and green for leaf. Stitch around outside of circle, turning edge under ½ inch as you stitch. Pull thread to gather.

13 Hem apron sides and bottom. Center apron along top of skirt. Gather skirt and apron at the same time and stitch to dress bodice. Stitch dress back ½ inch above waist to bottom of skirt.

14 Hem bottom of skirt, edge of sleeves, neck, and back opening.

15 Following manufacturer's directions, press fusible webbing to back of 2-inch squares of red and blue print fabrics. Trace and cut out small hearts. Peel off paper backing and press hearts to apron. Using black floss, stitch around hearts.

20 Stitch leaf and yoyo flower to heart. Stitch ½-inch round loop end of hook-and-loop tape to back of heart.

21 To make heart flag: Stitch 2 × 8-inch blue fabric to 3 × 8-inch red and white stripe.

22 Trace heart on wrong side of fabric, lining up seam line with seam. Fold fabric in half, right sides together. Layer 4-inch piece batting under 2 layers of fabric.

23 Stitch all the way around heart on traced line. Trim off excess fabric and batting. Clip curves and points. Take out enough stitches at seam of blue print fabric to turn. Turn right side out and stitch opening closed.

24 Stitch red, white, and blue buttons to front of heart flag. Stitch ½-inch round loop end of hook-and-loop tape to back of heart flag.

25 Use the same techniques to make a Christmas tree or Easter bunny. You can even make something special for Amber Lee to hold on Father's Day, Mother's Day, or an extra-special birthday!

Lo! the level lake
And the long glories of the winter
moon.

Alfred, Lord Tennyson
"Morte d'Arthur"

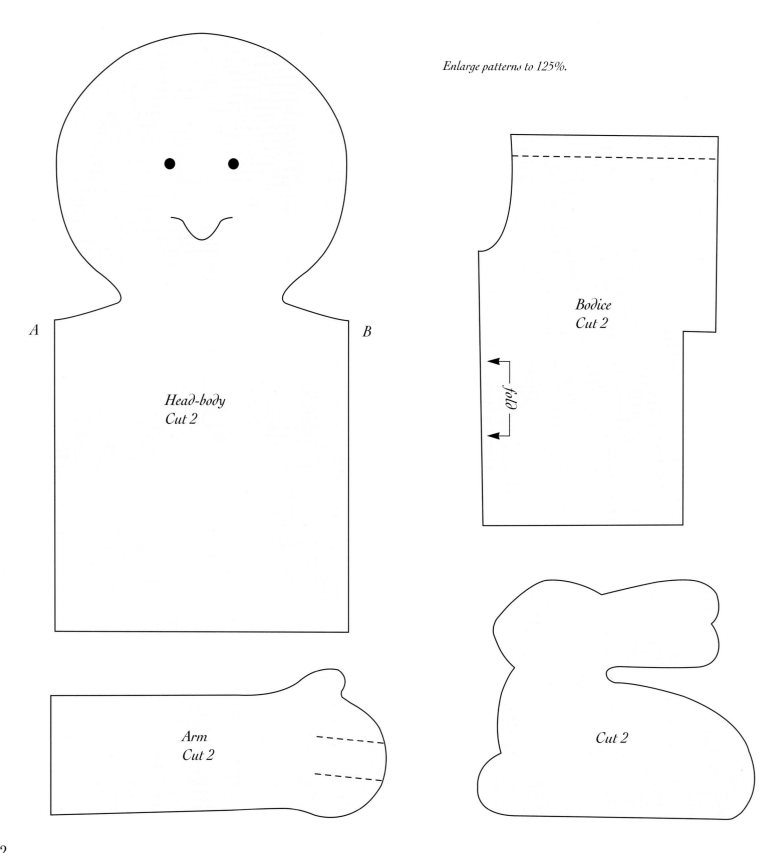

Enlarge patterns to 125%.

A

Head-body
Cut 2

B

Bodice
Cut 2

fold

Arm
Cut 2

Cut 2

62

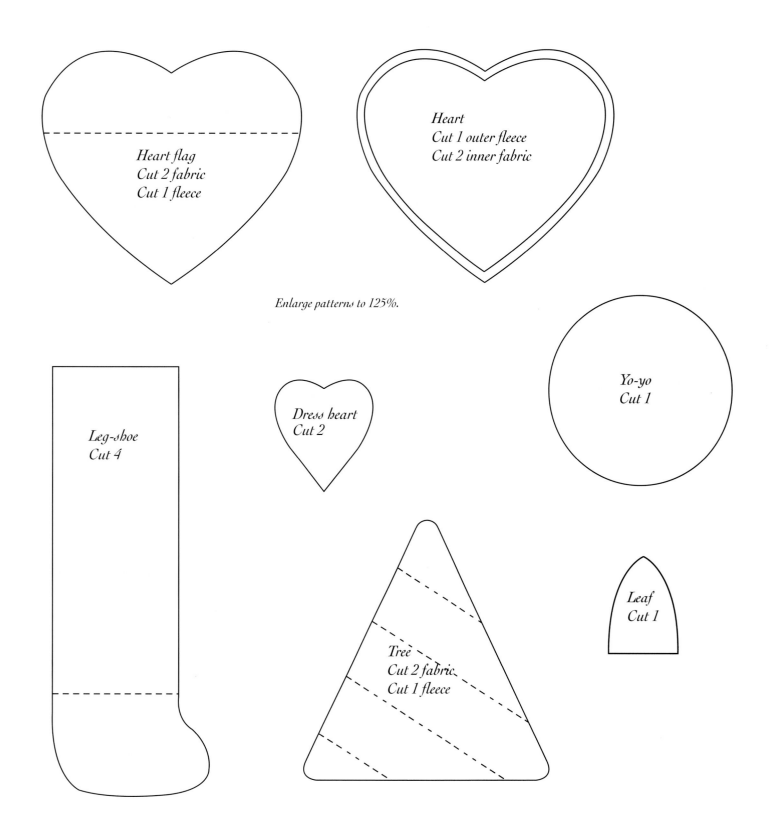

Heart flag
Cut 2 fabric
Cut 1 fleece

Heart
Cut 1 outer fleece
Cut 2 inner fabric

Enlarge patterns to 125%.

Leg-shoe
Cut 4

Dress heart
Cut 2

Yo-yo
Cut 1

Leaf
Cut 1

Tree
Cut 2 fabric
Cut 1 fleece

Santa's Special Delivery

♥

Whether hanging on a wall or laid across your comfy sofa, this Santa quilt is sure to catch everyone's eyes! The warmth of a homemade quilt is sure to take the chill out of the wintery air. ♥

WHAT YOU'LL NEED

1¾ yards background fabric

⅛ yard hat fabric

⅛ yard fur fabric

½ yard beard fabric

3-inch square face fabric

½ yard suit fabric

⅛ yard black fabric

Self-healing mat, rotary cutter, see-through ruler

Neutral thread for sewing

Black embroidery floss, embroidery needle

Small button

Blusher

⅛ yard star fabric

⅛ yard sled fabric

⅛ yard pot fabric

Scrap trunk fabric

¼ yard tree fabric

½ yard accent border fabric

½ yard each several colors of fabric

1 yard backing fabric

43 × 36-inch batting

1-inch safety pins

Washable marking pencil

⅓ yard binding fabric

Quilting thread

Quilting needle

1 Prewash and press all fabrics. For Santa block: You will assemble 1 row at a time. It is easiest to cut out and pile into rows. You may sew rows together as you go, or complete all 8 rows first. Rows 1 through 5 will measure 10½ inches wide. Rows 6 through 8 will measure 13 inches wide. (Where indicated, draw a diagonal line on the wrong side of the fabric.) First measurement given is always width of piece, second is always height of piece.

2 From background fabric cut a 3 × 10-inch strip. Row 1: From background fabric cut 10½ × 2½-inch strip. Row 2: From background fabric cut 3½ × 2-inch piece, 1½-inch square (diagonal), 5 × 2-inch piece; from hat fabric cut 4½ × 2-inch piece. Row 3: From background fabric cut two 2½ × 1½-inch pieces, 1-inch square (diagonal); from hat fabric cut 3½ × 1½-inch piece; from fur fabric cut 3½ × 1½-inch piece. Row 4: From background fabric cut 2½-inch square, 1½-inch square, 1½ × 2½-inch piece; from hat fabric cut 2½-inch square; from fur fabric cut 1½-inch square; from beard fabric cut 2½-inch square; from face fabric cut 2½-inch square; from suit fabric cut 1½-inch square (diagonal).

3 Row 5: From background fabric cut 2½-inch square (diagonal), two 2½ × 1½-inch pieces,

1½-inch square (diagonal), 1½ × 3½-inch piece; from beard fabric cut 4 × 3½-inch piece, 3 × 1½-inch piece, 2½-inch square (diagonal); from suit fabric cut 1½-inch square, 5 × 2½-inch piece. Row 6: From background fabric cut 2½-inch square, 3 × 1½-inch piece, two 1-inch squares (diagonals), 1½ × 3½-inch piece, 1½-inch square (diagonal); from beard fabric cut 3½ × 1½-inch piece, 4 × 2½-inch piece, 1-inch square (diagonal); from suit fabric cut 1-inch square (diagonal), 6½ × 3½-inch piece. Row 7: From background fabric cut 3 × 7½-inch piece, 1½ × 2½-inch piece, 1½-inch square, 3½ × 4½-inch piece; from fur fabric cut 7½ × 2½-inch piece; from suit fabric cut 7½ × 5½-inch piece, 2½-inch square; from black fabric cut 2½ × 1½-inch piece, 1½-inch square (diagonal). Row 8: From background fabric cut 2 × 3½-inch piece, two 1½-inch squares, 1½ × 3½-inch piece, 3½-inch square; from black fabric cut two 3 × 1½-inch pieces, two 4 × 2½-inch pieces.

4 Sew each row together in order. Unless otherwise indicated, all directions are right sides together with ¼-inch seam allowances. Row 1: Cut strip is full row. Row 2: Sew 1½-inch background square on diagonal to left top of 4½ × 2-inch hat piece. Cut fabric above seam. Lay the 5 × 2-inch background rectangle perpendicular on hat/background piece (right side of piece), and draw a diagonal (see diagram below, dashed line is cutting line). Sew on line and cut away fabric above seam. Sew 3½ × 2-inch background piece to left side of strip. Press seams.

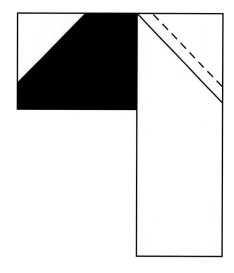

5 Row 3: Sew 1-inch background square to top right of 3½ × 1½-inch hat piece. Cut away fabric above seam. Sew a 2½ × 1½-inch background piece at right side of hat/background piece just sewn. To left of same piece, sew 3½ × 1½-inch fur piece, and to left of that sew 2½ × 1½-inch background piece. Row 4: Sew 1½-inch suit square on diagonal to bottom left of 2½-inch hat square. Cut away fabric below seam. Sew 1½-inch background square to top of 1½-inch fur square. To right of this piece, sew 1½ × 2½-inch background piece. Sew suit/hat piece to left of backround/fur piece. Sew 2½-inch beard square to left of suit/hat piece. Sew 2½-inch face square to left of beard square. Sew 2½-inch background square to left of face piece.

6 Row 5: Sew 2½-inch background square to top left of 4 × 3½-inch beard piece. Cut away fabric above seam. Sew 2½-inch beard square on diagonal to top left of 5 × 2½-inch suit piece. To same piece sew 1½-inch background square to top right. Cut away fabric above seam. To right of 3 × 1½-inch beard piece sew 1½-inch suit square and to right of that sew 2½ × 1½-inch background piece (this is piece A). Sew 2½ × 1½-inch background piece to right of beard/suit/background piece (this is piece B). Sew piece A to top of piece B. To right side of this (AB piece) sew 1½ × 3½-inch background piece. To left side of AB piece sew background/beard piece.

7 Sew bottom of row 1 to top of row 2. Sew bottom of row 2 to top of row 3. Continue until all 5 rows are sewn together. If you need to, lay out all rows so that the pattern emerges before sewing. Sew 3 × 10-inch background piece to left of rows 1–5 block.

8 Row 6: Sew a 1-inch background square on diagonal to the top left and another to the bottom left of 4 × 2½-inch beard piece. Cut fabric away above and below seam line. To same beard

piece sew 1-inch suit square to bottom right. Cut fabric away below seam line (piece A). Sew 1-inch beard square to top left of 6½ × 3½-inch suit piece. Cut fabric away above seam line. To same suit piece sew 1½-inch background square to top right side. Cut fabric away above seam line (piece B). Sew 3 × 1½-inch background piece to left side of 3½ × 1½-inch beard piece (piece C). Sew 2½-inch background square to piece A (piece D). Sew piece C to top of piece D. Sew CD to left side of piece B. Sew 1½ × 3½-inch background piece to right side of piece ABCD.

9 Row 7: Sew 1½-inch black square to bottom left of 1½ × 2½-inch background piece. Cut fabric away below seam line. Sew 7½ × 5½-inch suit piece to top of 7½ × 2½-inch fur piece. To left of this block sew 3 × 7½-inch background piece (this is piece A). Sew 2½-inch suit square to left side of black/background piece (this is piece B). Sew 1½-inch background square to left side of 2½ × 1½-inch black piece (this is piece C). Sew bottom of piece B to top of piece C. Sew bottom of piece BC to top of 3½ × 4½-inch background piece. To left of piece BC sew piece A.

10 Row 8: Sew 1½-inch background square to left side of 3 × 1½-inch black piece. Sew bottom of this piece to top of 4 × 2½-

inch black piece. Repeat. To left of first shoe block sew 2 × 3½-inch background piece. To right of same shoe block sew 1½ × 3½-inch background piece and to the right of that sew second shoe block. To right of this piece sew 3½-inch background square.

11 Sew bottom of row 6 to top of row 7 and bottom of row 7 to top of row 8. Sew bottom of rows 1–5 to top of rows 6–8. Using black embroidery floss, sew on small button for eye. Using finger, blush Santa's cheek.

12 You will make 10 star blocks. For star blocks: From background fabric cut eleven 4½ × 1-inch pieces, twenty 3 × 1½-inch pieces, forty 2 × 1½-inch pieces. From star fabric cut twenty 1½-inch squares (draw diagonal), ten 3½ × 1½-inch pieces.

13 Sew a 1½-inch star square to bottom right side of 3 × 1½-inch background piece. Cut fabric away below seam line. Make 20. Sew 2 × 1½-inch background piece to right side of star/background piece. Make 20. Sew a 2 × 1½-inch background piece to bot-

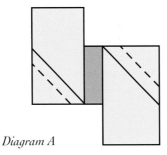

Diagram A

tom left and top right of a 3½ × 1½-inch star piece (see diagram A). Cut fabric away above and below seam lines where indicated. Make 10. Assemble stars as indicated in diagram B. Make 10. Sew 4½ × 1-inch background piece to tops of 7 stars. To bottoms of 4 of these stars sew 4½ × 1-inch background piece.

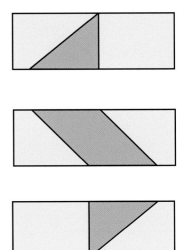

Diagram B

14 From background fabric cut a 2½ × 4-inch piece, 6½ × 10-inch piece, two 1½ × 3½-inch pieces. Sew a top-bordered star to left side of 2½ × 4-inch background piece (this is piece A). To either side of an unbordered star sew a 1½ × 3½-inch background piece (this is piece B). Sew bottom of piece A to top of piece B. Sew bottom of piece AB to top of 6½ × 10-inch background piece.

15 For sled and pot section: From background fabric cut 5½ × 2½-inch piece, 10 × 2-inch piece, $7\frac{1}{2} \times 2$-inch piece, $7 \times 1\frac{1}{2}$-inch piece, $4\frac{1}{2} \times 1\frac{1}{2}$-inch piece, $5 \times 2\frac{1}{2}$-inch piece, $2\frac{1}{2} \times 4\frac{1}{2}$-inch piece, $2\frac{1}{2}$-inch square (draw diagonal), $1\frac{1}{2}$-inch square, $1 \times 2\frac{1}{2}$-inch piece, $1\frac{1}{2} \times 2\frac{1}{2}$-inch piece. From sled fabric cut $1\frac{1}{2}$-inch square, $14\frac{1}{2} \times 2\frac{1}{2}$-inch piece. From pot fabric cut $7\frac{1}{2} \times 1\frac{1}{2}$-inch piece, $5\frac{1}{2} \times 2\frac{1}{2}$-inch piece. From trunk fabric cut $1\frac{1}{2} \times 2$-inch piece.

16 Sew $2\frac{1}{2}$-inch background square to bottom left of $14\frac{1}{2} \times 2\frac{1}{2}$-inch sled piece. Cut fabric away below seam line. To right side of this piece sew $1 \times 2\frac{1}{2}$-inch background piece. To left side of piece sew $1\frac{1}{2} \times 2\frac{1}{2}$-inch background piece (this is piece A). Sew $1\frac{1}{2}$-inch background square to top of $1\frac{1}{2}$-inch sled square. To right of this piece sew $5 \times 2\frac{1}{2}$-inch background piece. To right of this sew $5\frac{1}{2} \times 2\frac{1}{2}$-inch pot piece. To right of this sew $5\frac{1}{2} \times 2\frac{1}{2}$-inch background piece (this is piece B). Sew bottom of piece B to top of piece A. To left side of piece AB sew $2\frac{1}{2} \times 4\frac{1}{2}$-inch background piece. Sew $7 \times 1\frac{1}{2}$-inch background piece to left side of $7\frac{1}{2} \times 1\frac{1}{2}$-inch pot piece. To right of that sew $4\frac{1}{2} \times 1\frac{1}{2}$-inch background piece (this is piece C). To right side of 10×2-inch background piece sew $1\frac{1}{2} \times 2$-inch trunk piece. To right side of that sew $7\frac{1}{2} \times 2$-inch background piece (this is piece D). Sew bottom of piece D to top of piece C. Sew bottom of piece DC to top of piece AB. Embroider rope from Santa's hand to sled.

17 For tree section: From background fabric cut $12 \times 4\frac{1}{2}$-inch piece, $4 \times 12\frac{1}{2}$-inch piece, six $4\frac{1}{2}$-squares (draw diagonal). From tree fabric cut three $8\frac{1}{2} \times 4\frac{1}{2}$-inch pieces.

18 Sew a $4\frac{1}{2}$-inch background square on right side of $8\frac{1}{2} \times 4\frac{1}{2}$-inch tree square. Cut fabric away above seam. Repeat with $4\frac{1}{2}$-inch square on left side of same tree square. Make 3. Sew blocks on top of each other (3 high). Sew $4 \times 12\frac{1}{2}$-inch background piece to right side of tree blocks. Sew $12 \times 4\frac{1}{2}$-inch background piece to top of tree/background block.

19 Sew stars block to left side of tree block. Sew stars/tree block to top of sled block. Sew Santa block to left side of stars/tree/sled block.

20 From accent border fabric cut two $30\frac{1}{2} \times 1\frac{1}{2}$-inch strips, two $1\frac{1}{2} \times 25\frac{1}{2}$-inch strips. Sew $30\frac{1}{2} \times 1\frac{1}{2}$-inch strips to top and bottom of quilt. Sew $1\frac{1}{2} \times 25\frac{1}{2}$-inch stripes to right and left side of quilt.

21 Flying geese border: From background fabric cut a hundred $2\frac{1}{2}$-inch squares (draw diagonals). From multicolored fabrics cut fifty $4\frac{1}{2} \times 2\frac{1}{2}$-inch pieces. Sew a $2\frac{1}{2}$-inch square to right side of a $4\frac{1}{2} \times 2\frac{1}{2}$-inch piece. Cut fabric away above seam line. Repeat for left side. Make 50. Sew 16 blocks

together with points all going in same direction. Repeat. Sew 4 blocks together with points going up. Sew a star block to top of 4 geese blocks. Sew a 1-sided bordered star on top of unbordered star (with border between stars). Sew 5 geese blocks together with points going down. Sew to top of geese/stars strip. Sew a 2-sided bordered star to top and bottom of strip. Repeat.

22 Sew strip of 16 geese blocks to bottom and top of quilt. Sew stars/geese strips to right and left side of quilt.

23 Cut backing and batting 2 inches larger than quilt face. Place quilt face on top of backing and batting. Pin baste with 1-inch safety pins. Mark quilting design with washable marking pencil. Starting in center, quilt with small even stitches. Trim batting and backing even with quilt face.

24 For binding: Cut six $2\frac{1}{2}$-inch-wide strips width of fabric. Join all strips end to end. Follow instructions in Craft Techniques to finish binding.

Mocha Marshmallow Fudge

♥

1 tablespoon instant coffee
1 tablespoon boiling water
2½ cups sugar
½ cup butter or margarine
1 can (5 ounces) evaporated milk
  (⅔ cup)
1½ cups semisweet chocolate chips
1 jar (7 ounces) marshmallow creme
½ teaspoon vanilla extract

1 Line 9-inch-square baking pan with foil, extending edges over sides of pan. Lightly grease foil with butter. Dissolve coffee in water; set aside.

2 Place sugar, butter, and evaporated milk in 1-quart saucepan; bring to a boil over medium-high heat, stirring constantly. Reduce heat to medium. Continue boiling 5 minutes, stirring constantly. Remove from heat. Immediately stir in reserved coffee mixture, chocolate, marshmallow creme, and vanilla. Pour into prepared pan. Let stand 1 hour.

3 Lift candy out of pan using foil; remove foil. Cut into 1-inch squares. Cover; refrigerate until fudge is set.

Makes about 2½ pounds or 64 pieces

Chocolate Butter Crunch

♥

1 cup butter or margarine
1¼ cups sugar
¼ cup water
2 tablespoons light corn syrup
1 cup ground almonds, divided
½ teaspoon vanilla extract
¾ cup milk chocolate chips

1 Line 15½ × 10½ × 1-inch jelly-roll pan with foil, extending edges over sides of pan. Generously grease foil and a narrow metal spatula with butter.

2 Melt butter in 2-quart saucepan over medium heat. Add sugar, water, and corn syrup. Bring to a boil, stirring constantly.

3 Carefully clip the candy thermometer to side of pan (do not let bulb touch bottom of pan). Cook until thermometer registers 290°F, stirring frequently. Stir in ⅔ cup almonds and vanilla. Pour into prepared pan. Spread mixture into corners with prepared spatula. Let stand 1 minute. Sprinkle with chocolate chips. Let stand 2 to 3 minutes more until chocolate melts. Spread chocolate over candy. Sprinkle with remaining ⅓ cup almonds. Cool completely.

4 Lift candy out of pan using foil; remove foil. Break candy into pieces. Store in airtight container.

Makes about 1½ pounds

SPRING

WARMING BREEZES,
DELICATE FLOWERS
POKING UP FROM THE
COLD GROUND, SKIES
AFLUTTER WITH BIRDS—
ALL BODE THE ARRIVAL OF
SPRING, GLORIOUS
SPRING.

Family Quilt Plaque

WHAT YOU'LL NEED

14 × 14-inch plywood plaque

Sandpaper

Tack cloth

Stylus

Transfer paper

Acrylic paint: bluegrass, raspberry sherbert, Victorian rose, blue satin, spring rose, Indian sky, stoneware blue, Sedona clay, snow white, mink tan, buttermilk, black

Waterbase varnish

Ruler

Brushes: 10/0 liner, ½-inch flat, ¾-inch angle

Matte finishing spray

This quilt plaque is stitched with your love and paint.

STEP 1

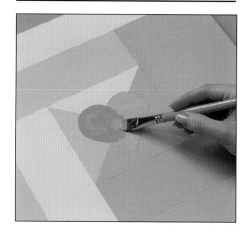

STEP 3

STEP 4

STEP 5

alternating rows offset; outer section has blue satin lines. Inside blue satin rectangle has buttermilk dots spaced ½ inch apart with alternating rows offset; outer section has buttermilk lines creating 1-inch squares. Inside Indian sky rectangle has buttermilk dot flowers and blue satin leaves; outer section has buttermilk ¾-inch squares with ¾-inch squares offset.

3 Float a shade on every fabric shape following inside edge with following colors: mink tan on buttermilk, bluegrass on blue satin, raspberry sherbert on spring rose, Sedona clay on Victorian rose, stoneware blue on Indian sky. Also base outermost edge of plaque with appropriate color.

4 Line all fabric pieces with snow white stitches. The beauty of quilting is keeping stitch lengths same as distance between stitches. Remember to use paint that is consistency of ink and to hold liner brush in an upright position.

5 Apply pattern for words and line with black. Dot letters with black using a pencil or stylus point.

6 After completely dry, spray with finishing spray.

1 Sand plaque and tack off excess dust with tack cloth. Apply pattern shapes to wood. Use equal parts of designated paint color and waterbase varnish for the first coat, and then paint only for repeated coats. The center heart is spring rose. See finished photo for placement of each color block.

2 Apply all fabric patterns. The small fabric pieces surrounding the heart and the heart have no patterns. Inside buttermilk rectangle has spring rose flower dots and blue satin leaves; outer buttermilk section has Indian sky lines. Inside Victorian rose rectangle has buttermilk dots spaced ½ inch apart with

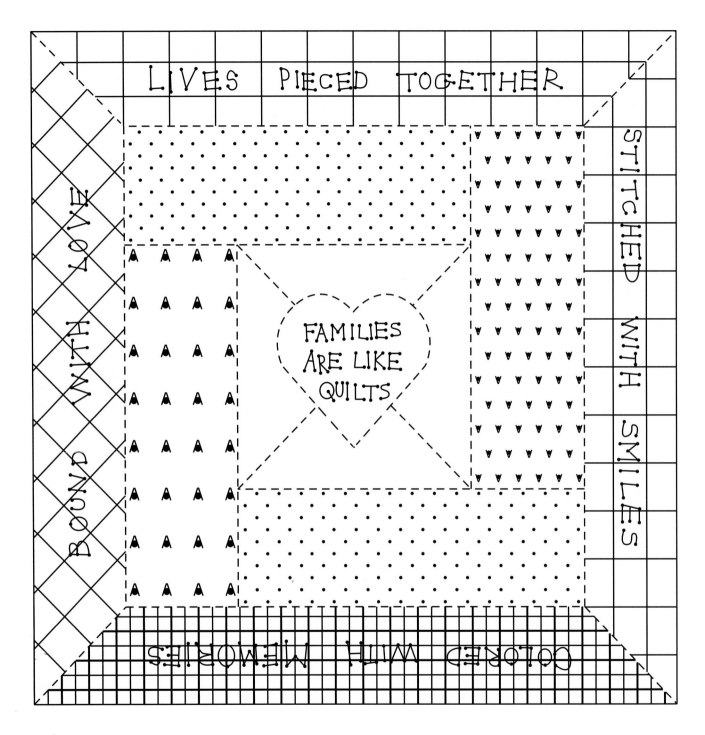

Enlarge pattern 200%.

76

Beef Tenderloin with Roasted Vegetables

♥

1 Place tenderloin in resealable plastic food bag. Combine chardonnay, soy sauce, garlic, rosemary, Dijon mustard, and dry mustard in bowl. Pour over tenderloin, turn to coat. Seal bag. Marinate in refrigerator 4 to 12 hours, turning several times.

2 Preheat oven to 425°F. Spray 13 × 9-inch baking pan with nonstick cooking spray. Place potatoes, brussels sprouts, and carrots in pan. Remove tenderloin from marinade. Pour marinade over vegetables; toss to coat. Cover vegetables with foil. Bake 30 minutes; stir. Place tenderloin on vegetables. Bake 40 minutes or until meat thermometer registers 135°F for rare, 155°F for medium, or 165°F for well. Remove tenderloin from pan and place on platter; tent with foil. Temperature of meat will increase about 5 degrees during 15-minute standing time.

3 Stir vegetables; test for doneness and continue to bake if not tender. Slice tenderloin; arrange on platter with vegetables. Garnish, if desired.

Makes 10 servings

1 beef tenderloin (3 pounds), well trimmed
½ cup chardonnay or other dry white wine
½ cup reduced sodium soy sauce
2 cloves garlic, sliced
1 tablespoon fresh rosemary

1 tablespoon Dijon mustard
1 teaspoon dry mustard
1 pound small red or white potatoes, cut into 1-inch pieces
1 pound brussels sprouts
12 ounces baby carrots

Basic White Bread

2 packages active dry yeast
2 tablespoons sugar
2 cups warm water (105°F to 115°F)
6 to 6½ cups all-purpose flour, divided
½ cup nonfat dry milk powder
2 tablespoons vegetable shortening
2 teaspoons salt

1 To proof yeast, sprinkle yeast and sugar over warm water in large bowl; stir until yeast is dissolved. Let stand 5 minutes or until mixture is bubbly.

2 Add 3 cups flour, nonfat dry milk powder, shortening, and salt. Beat with electric mixer at low speed until blended, scraping down side of bowl once. Increase speed to medium; beat 2 minutes, scraping down side of bowl once.

3 Stir in enough additional flour, about 3 cups, with wooden spoon to make soft dough.

4 Turn out dough onto lightly floured surface; flatten slightly. Knead dough about 10 minutes or until smooth and elastic, adding remaining ½ cup flour to prevent sticking if necessary.

5 Shape dough into a ball; place in a large greased bowl. Turn dough over so that top is greased. Cover with towel; let rise in warm place about 1 hour or until doubled in bulk.

6 Punch down dough. Knead dough on lightly floured surface 1 minute. Cover with towel; let rest 10 minutes.

7 Grease 2 (8½ × 4½-inch) loaf pans; set aside.

8 Divide dough in half. Roll out half of dough into 12 × 8-inch rectangle with lightly floured rolling pin. Starting with 8-inch side, roll up dough jelly-roll style. Pinch seam and ends to seal. Place loaf, seam side down, in prepared pan, tucking ends under. Repeat with remaining dough.

9 Cover with towel; let rise in warm place 1 hour or until doubled in bulk.

10 Preheat oven to 375°F. Bake 30 to 35 minutes or until loaves are golden brown and sound hollow when tapped. Immediately remove from pans; cool completely on wire racks.

REFRIGERATOR WHITE BREAD: Prepare and shape dough as directed in Steps 1 through 8. Spray 2 sheets of plastic wrap with nonstick cooking spray. Cover dough with plastic wrap, greased side down. Refrigerate 3 to 24 hours. Dough should rise to top of pans during refrigeration. Remove loaves from refrigerator 20 minutes before baking. Preheat oven to 375°F. Remove plastic wrap. Bake 45 to 50 minutes or until loaves are golden brown and sound hollow when tapped. Finish as directed in Step 10.

FREEZER WHITE BREAD: Prepare and shape dough as directed in Steps 1 through 8. Spray 2 sheets of plastic wrap with nonstick cooking spray. Cover dough with plastic wrap, greased side down. Freeze about 5 hours or until firm. Remove loaves from pans. Wrap frozen loaves securely in plastic wrap; place in labeled plastic freezer bags. Freeze up to 1 month. To bake loaves, unwrap and place in greased loaf pans. Cover with towel; let stand in warm place 4 to 5 hours or until loaves are thawed and doubled in bulk. Preheat oven to 375°F. Finish as directed above.

Wonderful Jumper

Denim jumper

4 coordinating fabrics for flowers, ⅛ yard each

Pencil

Scissors

Needle

Thread to match

Scraps of 1 or 2 green fabrics for leaves

4 battenburg doilies, 4 inches in diameter each

Washable fabric glue

1 cathedral-shaped doily (optional)

Sewing machine (optional)

Pins

9 small buttons to coordinate with flower fabrics

This stylish jumper is dressy, yet comfortable.♥

1 Trace a total of 9 circles for flower yo-yos onto coordinating fabrics and cut out. Trace and cut 10 circles from leaf fabrics.

2 With needle and thread, use a running stitch and stitch ⅛ inch from top of each flower fabric circle. Sew on wrong side of fabric. As you sew, pull or gather fabric. When completely around circle, pull thread tight and tie thread to secure. Flatten to form a fabric yo-yo.

3 Fold each leaf circle in half with right sides of material on outside. Fold the corners into the center and finger press in place.

4 With needle and thread, use a running stitch and stitch ⅛ inch from cut edges of leaves. Pull thread tight and secure with knot.

5 Lay jumper flat. Using photo as guide for placement, place battenburg doilies in appropriate positions. With washable fabric glue, secure doilies in place. Glue along all solid edges of doilies to secure bond. (If cathedral doily is to be used as a pocket on lower right of jumper, sew in place with machine.)

6 Lay out yo-yo flowers and leaves. Pin and then sew in place using needle and thread. Blindstitch around outside edge of each flower, tucking the leaves underneath the flowers.

7 Sew a button in center of each flower.

Tip: If you do not have the desired colors in your scraps of fabric, or you just wish to take a shortcut, you can purchase premade cloth yo-yos at most craft or fabric stores.

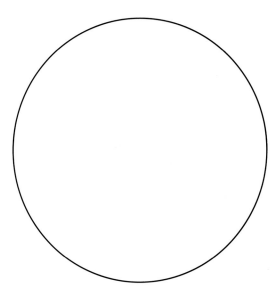

Pattern is 100%.

Vegetable Tart

♥

Pastry Dough (recipe follows)
Olive oil flavored nonstick
    cooking spray
1 small sweet potato
1 tablespoon olive or vegetable
    oil
1 cup sliced mushrooms
½ cup thinly sliced leeks
1 medium zucchini, sliced
1 parsnip, sliced
1 medium red bell pepper, cut
    into 1-inch pieces
8 to 10 cloves garlic, minced
1 teaspoon dried basil leaves
½ teaspoon dried rosemary
½ teaspoon salt
    Black pepper (optional)
2 to 4 tablespoons grated
    Parmesan cheese
1 egg white, beaten

1 Preheat oven to 400°F. Prepare Pastry Dough. While dough is resting, begin preparing vegetables for tart.

2 Spray nonstick baking sheet with cooking spray. Slice sweet potato into ¼-inch-thick slices. Place on prepared baking sheet; spray tops of slices with cooking spray. Bake 15 to 20 minutes or until potatoes are tender, turning slices once.

3 Heat oil in large skillet over medium heat until hot. Add mushrooms, leeks, zucchini, parsnip, bell pepper, garlic, basil, and rosemary; cook and stir 8 to 10 minutes or until vegetables are tender. Season to taste with salt and black pepper, if desired.

4 Roll out Pastry Dough on lightly floured surface to a 14-inch round; place on cookie sheet or large pizza pan. Place sweet potato slices evenly over crust, leaving a 2½-inch border around side. Spoon vegetable mixture evenly over potatoes; sprinkle with cheese. Fold edge of dough over edge of vegetable mixture, pleating dough as necessary to fit. Brush edge of dough with egg white.

5 Bake 25 minutes or until pastry is golden brown. Garnish with fresh basil and rosemary, if desired. Cut into wedges; serve warm.

Makes 16 servings

PASTRY DOUGH

1 teaspoon active dry yeast
⅓ cup warm water (115°F)
1 egg, beaten
3 tablespoons nonfat sour
    cream
1¼ cups all-purpose flour
¼ cup whole wheat flour
¼ teaspoon salt

To proof yeast, sprinkle over warm water in medium bowl; stir until yeast is dissolved. Let stand 5 minutes or until mixture is bubbly. Add egg and sour cream, mixing until smooth. Stir in flours and salt, making soft dough. Knead dough on lightly floured surface 1 to 2 minutes or until smooth. Shape dough into ball; place in large bowl sprayed with olive oil flavored nonstick cooking spray. Turn dough over to grease top. Cover bowl with towel; let rest in warm place 20 minutes.

Makes pastry for 1 tart

Fudgy Bittersweet Brownie Pie

12 ounces bittersweet
   chocolate candy bar,
   broken into pieces
½ cup butter or margarine
2 large eggs
½ cup sugar

1 cup all-purpose flour
½ teaspoon salt
  Vanilla ice cream
  Prepared hot fudge sauce
  Red and white candy
    sprinkles for garnish

1 Preheat oven to 350°F. Grease 10-inch tart pan with removable bottom; set aside.

2 Melt chocolate and butter in heavy saucepan over low heat, stirring constantly; set aside.

3 Beat eggs in medium bowl with electric mixer at medium speed 30 seconds. Gradually beat in sugar; beat 1 minute. Beat in chocolate mixture, scraping down side of bowl once. Beat in flour and salt at low speed until just combined, scraping down side of bowl once. Spread batter evenly in pan.

4 Bake 25 minutes or until center is just set. Remove pan to wire rack; cool completely.

5 To serve, cut brownies into 12 wedges, or 12 squares if using square pan. Top each piece with a scoop of vanilla ice cream. Place fudge sauce in small microwavable bowl or glass measuring cup. Microwave at HIGH until hot, stirring once. Spoon over ice cream; top with candy sprinkles.

6 Store brownies tightly covered at room temperature or freeze up to 3 months.

Makes 16 brownies

Cross-Stitch Pillow

WHAT YOU'LL NEED

Premade pillow

Embroidery floss (see color chart)

Embroidery needle

Scissors

Pillow form

Small button

T his whimsical pillow hosts a cast of colorful country characters. ♥

All cross-stitch is done with 4 strands floss and all backstitch is done with 3 strands. Backstitch bunny with black, birdhouse and flower with light brown, and bird with dark blue. Sew button on top right heart.

Color	DMC		Color	DMC
Brick	3722		Black	310
Light green	368		White	White
Dark green	367		Light rose	224
Yellow	3822		Dark rose	3721
Orange	977		Light brown	436
Light blue	931		Dark brown	434
Dark blue	930		Ecru	822

86

Sugar Cookies

♥

These delicious cookies can be decorated to represent all the colors of spring! ♥

1 cup sugar
1 cup butter or margarine
2 eggs
½ teaspoon lemon extract
½ teaspoon vanilla
3 cups all-purpose flour, divided
1 teaspoon baking powder
¼ teaspoon salt
    Egg Yolk Paint (recipe
      follows)
    Royal Icing (recipe follows)
    Decorator Frosting (recipe
      follows)

EQUIPMENT AND DECORATIONS:
    Liquid or paste food coloring
    Small paint brushes
    Sponges

1 Beat sugar and butter in large bowl with electric mixer at medium speed until light and fluffy. Beat in eggs and extracts at medium speed until well blended, scraping down side of bowl occasionally (mixture will look grainy). Beat in 1 cup flour, baking powder, and salt at medium speed until well blended. Gradually add remaining 2 cups flour. Beat at low speed until soft dough forms, scraping down side of bowl once.

2 Form dough into 3 discs. Wrap discs in plastic wrap; refrigerate 2 hours or until dough is firm.

3 Preheat oven to 375°F. Working with 1 disc at a time, unwrap dough and place on lightly floured surface. Roll out dough with lightly floured rolling pin to ⅛-inch thickness.

4 Cut dough with lightly floured 3- to 4-inch cookie cutters. Place cutouts 1 inch apart on ungreased cookie sheets. Gently press dough trimmings together; reroll and cut out more cookies. (If dough is sticky, pat into disc; wrap in plastic wrap and refrigerate until firm before rerolling.)

5 To paint cookies before baking, prepare Egg Yolk Paint. Divide paint among several bowls; tint with liquid food coloring, if desired.

6 Paint yolk paint onto unbaked cookies with paint brush.

7 Bake 7 to 9 minutes or until cookies are set. Remove cookies with spatula to wire rack; cool completely.

8 To sponge paint cooled cookies, prepare Royal Icing. Divide

icing among several bowls; tint with liquid or paste food coloring. For best results, use 2 to 3 shades of the same color. (If icing is too thick, stir in water, 1 drop at a time, with spoon until slightly thinned.)

9 Spread thin layer of icing on cookies to within ⅛ inch of edges with small spatula. Let stand 30 minutes at room temperature or until icing is set.

10 Cut clean kitchen sponge into 1-inch squares with scissors. Dip sponge into tinted icing, scraping against side of bowl to remove excess icing. Gently press sponge on base icing several times until desired effect is achieved. Let stand 15 minutes or until icing is set.

11 To pipe additional decorations on cookies, prepare Decorator Frosting. Tint frosting as directed in Step 8, if desired.

12 Place each color frosting in piping bag fitted with small writing tip or resealable plastic freezer bags with a small corner cut off. Decorate as desired. Let cookies stand at room temperature until piping is set.

13 Store loosely covered at room temperature up to 1 week.

Makes about 3 dozen cookies

EGG YOLK PAINT

  2 egg yolks
  2 teaspoons water

Combine egg yolks and water in small bowl with fork until blended.

Makes about ⅓ cup

Note: Only brush this paint onto unbaked cookies.

DECORATOR FROSTING

  ¾ cup butter, softened
 4½ cups powdered sugar, sifted, divided
  3 tablespoons water
  1 teaspoon vanilla
  ¼ teaspoon lemon extract

Beat butter in medium bowl with electric mixer at medium speed until smooth. Add 2 cups sugar. Beat at medium speed until light and fluffy. Add water and extracts. Beat at low speed until well blended, scraping down side of bowl once. Beat in remaining 2½ cups sugar until mixture is creamy.

Makes 2 cups

Note: This frosting is perfect for piping, but is less durable than Royal Icing. Bumping, stacking, and handling may damage decorations.

ROYAL ICING

  4 egg whites*
  4 cups powdered sugar, sifted
  1 teaspoon lemon extract or clear vanilla extract**

*Use only grade A clean, uncracked eggs.
**Icing remains very white when clear flavorings are used.

Beat egg whites in clean, large bowl with electric mixer at high speed until foamy. Gradually add sugar and lemon extract. Beat at high speed until thickened.

Makes 2 cups

Note: When dry, Royal Icing is very hard and resistant to damage that can occur during shipping.

Spring Brunch Table Runner

♥

This festive table runner is sure to make your spring brunch the hit of the ladies club or your family party! ♥

Approximate size 24 × 50½-inches

WHAT YOU'LL NEED

⅙ **yard pink fabric**

½ **yard green fabric**

⅓ **yard blue fabric**

⅝ **yard cream fabric**

½ **yard print fabric**

Sewing machine

Pins

Thread: nylon, cream

Rotary cutter, self-healing mat, see-through ruler

1½ **yards batting**

1½ **yards backing fabric**

1 Prewash and press all fabrics. This project is assembled using template-free rotary cutting. The first cut is always from selvage to selvage.

2 Label each piece after cutting as indicated. From pink fabric: Cut a strip 4½ inches wide, from that strip cut three 4½-inch squares (piece E). Trim remainder of strip to 3¼ inches wide, from that strip cut six 3¼-inch squares. Cut these squares in half diagonally (piece C).

3 From green fabric: Cut a strip 5½ inches wide, from that strip cut three 5½-inch squares. Cut these squares in quarters diagonally (piece D). For inner border: Cut 3 strips 1 inch wide; 2 strips 1 × 41½ inches and 2 strips 1 × 16 inches. For binding: Cut 4 strips 2 inches wide.

4 From blue fabric: Cut 2 strips 5¼ inches wide, from these strips cut twelve 5¼-inch squares. Cut these in half diagonally, then trim each triangle to a 2-inch trapezoid (piece B). (To cut trapezoid, place the 2-inch line of a ruler along the long edge of piece B and trim the triangle above 2-inch line.)

5 From cream fabric: Cut a strip 5½ inches wide, from this strip cut three 5½-inch squares. Cut these squares in quarters diagonally (piece D). Trim remainder of strip to 3¼ inches, from this strip cut six 3¼-inch squares. Cut squares in half diagonally (piece C). Cut a strip 5¼ inches wide, from this strip cut six 5¼-inch squares. Cut these squares in half diagonally (piece A). Cut 4 strips 1¾ inches wide, from this strip cut 6 strips: 2 strips 1¾ × 39 inches, 2 strips 1¾ × 12½ inches, 2 strips 1¾ × 15 inches.

6 From print fabric: Cut 4 strips 4 inches wide. Cut 2 strips 4 × 42½ inches and 2 strips 4 × 23 inches. If your fabric measures less than 42½ inches wide you will have to piece side borders.

7 To construct corner units: Sew 12 cream A pieces to 12 blue B pieces along longest edges. Sew 12 cream C pieces to each unit to form squares. Press seams toward cream pieces. Trim units to 4½-inch square. (To square unit: Use a 6-inch bias square ruler. Place diagonal [45 degree line] along

diagonal seam line and trim 2 sides, making sure that there is more than a 4½-inch square remaining. Turn unit and realign ruler with 4½-inch mark on 2 trimmed sides and trim remaining sides.)

8 To construct side units: Sew 12 cream D pieces to 12 green D pieces. Press seam toward green. Sew 12 pink C pieces to 12 blue B pieces to form large triangle. Sew these 2 units together along longest edges. Press toward blue. Trim units to 4½-inch square. (Trim for the corner unit; the center of square aligns with 2¼-inch mark on ruler.)

9 Make 3 blocks with pink piece E as center of each. (If needed, see finished photo for placement.)

10 To make lattice: Sew two 12½-inch cream strips to 2 blocks; sew blocks together (block-lattice-block-lattice-block). Sew a 39-inch lattice to each side; then sew a 15-inch lattice strip to top and bottom.

11 To make borders: Sew side borders (42½-inch pieces) on first; then sew on top and bottom.

12 To finish: Cut backing fabric and batting about 2 inches larger than quilt face. Layer top, batting, and backing fabric; then baste. Quilt as desired by machine or hand. Bind (see Craft Techniques for instructions).

Ham and Cheese Bread Pudding

♥

1 small loaf (8 ounces) sourdough, country French, or Italian bread
3 tablespoons butter or margarine, softened
8 ounces ham or smoked ham, cubed
2 cups (8 ounces) shredded mild or sharp Cheddar cheese
3 eggs
2 cups milk
1 teaspoon dry mustard
½ teaspoon salt
⅛ teaspoon white pepper
Green bell pepper rings and red bell pepper strips for garnish

1 Preheat oven to 350°F. Grease 11 × 7-inch baking dish; set aside.

2 Trim ends from bread with serrated knife; discard. Cut bread into 1-inch-thick slices. Spread 1 side of each bread slice with butter. Stack 2 slices at a time. Make lengthwise cuts 1 inch apart, then make crosswise cuts, cutting bread into 1-inch cubes. Repeat with remaining bread slices.

3 Spread bread cubes in bottom of prepared dish. Top with ham; sprinkle with cheese.

4 Beat eggs in medium bowl with wire whisk. Whisk in milk, mustard, salt, and pepper. Pour egg mixture evenly over bread mixture. Cover; refrigerate at least 6 hours or overnight.

5 Bake bread pudding uncovered 45 to 50 minutes or until puffed and golden brown, and knife inserted in center comes out clean. Garnish, if desired. Cut into squares. Serve immediately.

Makes 8 servings

Sour Cream Coffee Cake

♥

Streusel Topping
(recipe follows)
1 lemon
¾ cup sugar
6 tablespoons butter or
margarine
2 eggs
1 cup sour cream
1½ teaspoons vanilla
1½ cups all-purpose flour
1½ teaspoons ground cardamon
1 teaspoon baking powder
1 teaspoon baking soda
⅛ teaspoon salt
Cranberry Sauce (recipe
follows)

1 Prepare Streusel Topping. Set aside. Grease and flour bottom and side of 8-inch springform pan.

2 Finely grate colored portion of lemon peel using bell grater or handheld grater. Measure 1 tablespoon lemon peel.

3 Preheat oven to 350°F. Beat sugar and butter in large bowl with electric mixer at medium speed until light and fluffy, scraping down side of bowl once. Beat in eggs, 1 at a time, until well blended. Beat in sour cream, vanilla, and lemon peel. Add flour, cardamon, baking powder, baking soda, and salt; beat at low speed just until blended, scraping down side of bowl occasionally.

4 Spoon half of batter into prepared pan. Sprinkle half of streusel over batter. Repeat layers ending with streusel.

5 Bake 50 to 60 minutes or until wooden pick inserted in center comes out clean. Cool in pan on wire rack 15 minutes. Run knife around edge of pan to loosen cake. Unhinge side; lift off. Cool until cake is just warm to touch.

6 Slide knife under cake; rotate cake to loosen. Slide onto serving plate. Serve cake with Cranberry Sauce.

7 Wrap in plastic wrap. Store at room temperature 1 week.

Makes 10 servings

STREUSEL TOPPING
¾ cup chopped walnuts
⅓ cup packed light brown sugar
2 tablespoons all-purpose flour
½ teaspoon ground cardamon
½ teaspoon ground nutmeg
½ teaspoon ground cinnamon
3 tablespoons butter, melted

Combine walnuts, sugar, flour, cardamon, nutmeg, and cinnamon in small bowl. Stir in butter until well blended.

Makes about ¾ cup

CRANBERRY SAUCE
2 cups fresh or thawed frozen
cranberries, drained
1 cup orange juice
¾ cup sugar
2 teaspoons cornstarch
2 teaspoons water
1 tablespoon grated lemon peel
2 to 3 tablespoons cranberry-
or orange-flavored liqueur
(optional)

1 Combine cranberries, orange juice, and sugar in saucepan. Bring to a boil stirring often with wooden spoon. Cover; simmer 10 minutes or until cranberries are tender and pop. Remove saucepan from heat.

2 Reserve ½ of cranberries. Mash remaining cranberries.

3 Blend cornstarch and water until smooth. Add to saucepan with lemon peel; blend.

4 Simmer mixture over medium heat 2 minutes or until thickened, stirring frequently. Stir in reserved whole cranberries. Remove saucepan from heat. Cool completely. Stir in liqueur.

5 Store in airtight container in refrigerator up to 3 weeks.

Makes about 2 cups

Morning Glory Birdhouse

♥

WHAT YOU'LL NEED

36 × 3½-inch stained fence post

4 × 6-inch stained birdhouse

Hot glue gun, glue sticks

Wire cutters

6 stems preserved plumosus fern

Staple gun, staples

6-foot silk blue morning glory vine garland

6 to 8 stems honeysuckle garland vine

Sheet moss

Hammer and nails (optional)

What a charming way to welcome your guests with this rustic-looking birdhouse. ♥

S T E P 2	S T E P 3	S T E P 4

1 Hot glue or nail birdhouse 11 inches from top of fence post.

2 Cut and hot glue fern up fence post and around birdhouse.

3 Staple morning glory vine up fence post and around birdhouse, facing flowers in different directions for a more natural look.

4 Hot glue honeysuckle vine pieces and moss throughout arrangement.

There was only — spring itself; the throb of it, the light restlessness, the vital essence of it everywhere: in the sky, in the swift clouds, in the pale sunshine, and in the warm, high wind — rising suddenly, sinking suddenly, impulsive and playful like a big puppy that pawed you and then lay down to be petted.

Willa Cather
My Ántonia

Hot Cross Buns

♥

4½ to 5 cups all-purpose flour, divided
½ cup granulated sugar
2 packages active dry yeast
1 teaspoon salt
1½ cups plus 1 tablespoon milk, divided
½ cup butter or margarine
3 eggs, divided
1 cup raisins
1 tablespoon water
¾ cup sifted powdered sugar
½ teaspoon vanilla

1 Combine 2 cups flour, granulated sugar, yeast, and salt in large bowl.

2 Combine 1½ cups milk and butter in 1-quart saucepan. Heat over low heat until mixture is 120°F to 130°F. (Butter does not need to completely melt.)

3 Gradually beat milk mixture into flour mixture with electric mixer at low speed. Increase speed to medium; beat 2 minutes, scraping down side of bowl once.

4 Reduce speed to low. Beat in 2 eggs and 1½ cups flour. Increase speed to medium; beat 2 minutes, scraping down side of bowl once.

5 Stir in raisins and enough additional flour, about 1 cup, with wooden spoon to make soft dough.

6 Turn out dough onto lightly floured surface; flatten slightly. Knead dough 8 to 10 minutes or until smooth and elastic, adding remaining ½ cup flour to prevent sticking if necessary.

7 Shape dough into a ball; place in large greased bowl. Turn dough over so that top is greased. Cover with towel; let rise in warm place about 1 hour or until doubled in bulk.

8 Punch down dough. Knead dough on lightly floured surface 1 minute. Cover with towel; let rest 10 minutes.

9 Grease 2 (8 × 8-inch) square baking pans or 13 × 9-inch baking pan.

10 Cut dough into 18 pieces. Shape each piece into a ball. Place balls in rows in prepared pans.

11 Cover with towel; let rise in warm place about 45 minutes or until doubled in bulk.

12 Preheat oven to 350°F. Beat remaining egg and 1 tablespoon water in small bowl.

13 Cut a cross in top of each bun with tip of sharp knife.

14 Brush rolls with egg mixture.

15 Place pieces of waxed paper under wire racks to keep counter clean; set aside.

16 Bake 20 to 25 minutes or until buns are golden brown and sound hollow when tapped. Immediately remove from pans; cool on wire racks while preparing icing.

17 To make icing, combine powdered sugar, vanilla, and remaining 1 tablespoon milk in small bowl until smooth. Spoon into decorating bag fitted with medium writing tip (#8). If using disposable decorating bag, cut pointed end so that opening is about ¼ inch wide. Fill cross in each bun with icing.

Makes 18 buns

Peach Terra-Cotta Garden

5 × 5 × 10-inch oval terra-cotta container

Hot glue gun, glue sticks

3 × 4 × 8-inch block dry floral foam

Wire cutters

10 to 12 stems dried green and blue hydrangea

18 to 20 dried peach roses

12 stems fresh or dried peach and mauve statice

5 to 6 stems dried pink celosia

3 ounces dried white larkspur

Green floral tape

2½-inch floral wood picks

6 stems fresh or dried lemon leaf (salal)

1 ounce dried festuca grass

T*he beauty of a sun-soaked garden is captured in this terra-cotta arrangement.* ♥

STEP 1

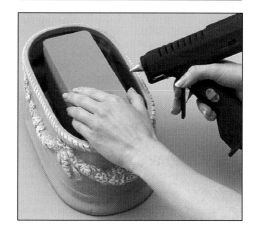

STEP 2

STEP 3

STEP 4

1 Hot glue foam into center of container.

2 Cut stems of hydrangea 8 to 10 inches long and insert into foam at center and around the edges of container.

3 Cut dried roses, statice, celosia, and larkspur 7 to 10 inches. Attach floral tape-wrapped wood pick to bundles and insert bundles throughout container.

4 Hot glue lemon leaf and festuca grass into any open areas around bottom and top of arrangement.

*In the dooryard fronting an old farm-
    house near the white-washed palings,
Stands the lilac-bush tall-growing with
    heart-shaped leaves of rich green,
With many a pointed blossom rising
    delicate, with the perfume strong I love,
With every leaf a miracle—and from this
    bush in the dooryard,
With delicate-color'd blossoms and heart-
    shaped leaves of rich green,
A sprig with its flower I break.*

*Walt Whitman
"When Lilacs Last in the Dooryard
Bloom'd"*

Favorite Beef Stew

♥

1 Cut beef into ¾-inch cubes, trimming off and discarding fat. Place meat in large bowl; sprinkle with flour, salt, and pepper. Toss lightly to coat.

2 Heat oil in 5-quart Dutch oven over medium-high heat. Add meat; brown, stirring frequently.

3 Add beef stock, tomatoes with liquid, garlic, bay leaf, Worcestershire, thyme, and basil; bring to a boil over high heat. Reduce heat to low; simmer, uncovered, 1½ hours, stirring occasionally.

4 Meanwhile, to cube potatoes, peel potatoes, then cut each into ½-inch-thick slices. Stack several slices and cut lengthwise into ½-inch strips. Then cut crosswise into ½-inch pieces. Place potatoes in large bowl and cover with water.

5 Increase heat to medium. Drain potatoes. Add potatoes, onions, carrots, and celery; heat until boiling. Reduce heat to low; simmer, uncovered, 30 minutes or until meat and vegetables are tender. Ladle into bowls. Garnish, if desired.

Makes 6 servings

1½ pounds beef stew meat
3 tablespoons all-purpose flour
1 teaspoon salt
½ teaspoon ground black pepper
2 tablespoons vegetable oil
1 cup beef stock or canned beef broth
1 can (16 ounces) whole tomatoes, cut-up, undrained
1 clove garlic, minced
1 bay leaf
1 tablespoon Worcestershire sauce
½ teaspoon dried thyme leaves, crushed
¼ teaspoon dried basil leaves, crushed
2 potatoes
1 cup frozen pearl onions
2 carrots, cut into ½-inch pieces
2 ribs celery, cut into ½-inch pieces
Onion rings and fresh herb leaves for garnish

Country Heart Sachet

♥

A𝒹𝒹 a touch of fragrance to your home with a country heart sachet. Elegant silk ribbon emroidery graces the felt heart. ♥

WHAT YOU'LL NEED

6 × 6-inch tear-away

Water-erasable marker

Scissors

9 × 12-inch felt pieces: ½ piece Wedgewood blue, ½ piece antique white

Pins

Silk or silklike embroidery ribbon (see color key)

#20 chenille needle

6-strand cotton embroidery floss: ecru, pink (DMC 3688)

Potpourri

8-inch length dusty rose ribbon, ⅜ inch wide

⁷⁄₁₆-inch sew-through button

1 Trace entire pattern onto tear-away. Using marker to trace around pattern, cut 2 larger hearts of Wedgewood blue felt. Trim pattern piece along smaller heart outline. Cut smaller heart of antique white felt. Pin or baste tear-away pattern to antique white heart. Work ribbon embroidery through tear-away.

2 Work ribbon embroidery according to photo and diagrams. Use 2 strands ecru floss to work spokes for spider web rose. Stitch flowers, then vine. Add leaves and French knots last. Remove pattern by gently tearing away from under stitching.

3 Center and pin embroidered heart on a blue heart. Attach white heart to blue by blanket stitching with 6 strands pink floss.

4 Blanket stitch blue hearts together with 6 strands ecru floss. Pause about ¾ of way around. Fill with potpourri then continue joining hearts.

5 Fold ribbon in half, turning ends up about ½ inch. Position on back of stuffed heart at top center with folded ends against felt. Use 6 strands ecru floss to tack ribbon hanger to heart and to sew button on front.

Ribbon			
Color		**YLI**	**Width**
▬ Dark green		021	4mm
▬ Light green		060	4mm
▬ Gold		54	4mm
▬ Rose		113	4mm
▬ Blue		126	7mm

∅∅	Lazy Daisy
——	Stem Stitch
⬭	Japanese Ribbon Stitch
• •	French Knot
✳	Loop Flower
◯	Spider Web Rose

Pattern is 100%.

SUMMER

SOFT HUMMING OF

BUMBLEBEES, MUSIC OF

FALLING WATER

QUENCHING THE THIRSTY

LAWN, BUBBLING OF

CHILDREN'S LAUGHTER—

OH HOW MANY SUMMER

PLEASURES ARE THERE?

Antique Watering Can

♥

WHAT YOU'LL NEED

Antique watering can

3 × 4 × 8-inch block dry floral foam

Hot glue gun, glue sticks

Wire cutters

3 ounces dried white larkspur

3 ounces dried nigella

3 ounces dried oregano

7 to 8 stems dried cream roses

5 stems dried dark pink roses

2 to 3 stems dried blue and green hydrangea

This elegant watering can creates a new country look with roses, larkspur, and hydrangeas. ♥

STEP 1

STEP 2

STEP 3

STEP 4

Now the summer came to pass
And flowers through the grass
Joyously sprang,
While all the tribes of birds sang.

Walther von der Vogelweide
"Dream Song"

1 Cut and hot glue foam up to lip of watering can.

2 Cut larkspur, nigella, and oregano 10 to 15 inches long. Insert groups at center of can behind the handle. Insert larkspur in center first.

3 Cut dried roses 4 to 8 inches long and insert cream roses in center in front of handle and pink roses at base.

4 Cut hydrangea 3 to 4 inches long and insert around edges of container, securing with hot glue if necessary.

Buttermilk Pancakes with Blueberry-Orange Sauce

Blueberry-Orange Sauce
(recipe follows)
2 cups all-purpose flour
1 tablespoon sugar
1½ teaspoons baking powder
½ teaspoon baking soda
½ teaspoon salt
1 egg
1½ cups buttermilk
¼ cup vegetable oil

1 Prepare Blueberry-Orange Sauce. Lightly grease and preheat griddle or large skillet over medium heat.

2 Combine flour, sugar, baking powder, baking soda, and salt in large bowl.

3 Place egg in medium bowl; beat with wire whisk. Gradually add buttermilk and oil, whisking continuously until mixture is thoroughly blended.

4 Stir egg mixture into flour mixture just until moistened.

5 For each pancake, pour about ½ cup batter onto hot griddle. Cook until tops of pancakes appear dry; turn with spatula and continue cooking 2 minutes or until golden brown. Serve with Blueberry-Orange Sauce.

Makes 6 to 8 (5-inch) pancakes

BLUEBERRY-ORANGE SAUCE
2 tablespoons cornstarch
2 tablespoons cold water
½ cup orange juice
1 tablespoon grated orange peel
1 bag (16 ounces) frozen
    blueberries, thawed, or 3½
    to 4 cups fresh blueberries
½ cup sugar
2 tablespoons orange-flavored
    liqueur

1 Stir cornstarch into water in medium saucepan until smooth. Stir in orange juice and orange peel.

2 Add blueberries, any accumulated juices, and sugar to cornstarch mixture. Cook and stir over high heat until mixture comes to a boil. Reduce heat to medium-low and simmer 2 to 3 minutes (4 to 5 minutes for fresh blueberries) or until mixture thickens, stirring occasionally. Remove from heat and stir in liqueur. Serve immediately.

Makes 6 to 8 servings (about 2¾ cups)

Flag Fanfare

♥

Celebrate your love for America with an Americana classic—a flag quilt! It truly conveys the pioneer spirit. ♥

There is no season such delight can bring,
As summer, autumn, winter, and the spring.

William Brown
"Variety"

1 For center star section: Cut 20 red 2 × 2-inch squares and 16 white 3½ × 2-inch rectangles. Draw a diagonal line corner to corner on the wrong side of 16 red squares.

2 (Unless otherwise noted, all seam allowances are ¼ inch and all pieces are matched right sides together. After sewing, press all seams to darkest fabric.) Lay a 2-inch red diagonal-marked square on the right side of a 3½ × 2-inch white rectangle. Sew along diagonal and trim fabric ½ inch away from seam line. Make 16 pieces.

3 Following diagram below, sew piece A to top of B. Sew piece C to top of AB. Sew piece E to bottom left of piece B and bottom of A. Sew piece D to top left of piece E and left of piece AC. Sew 4 star blocks together to make a large block.

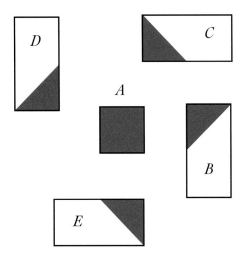

4 For flag: Cut 4 blue 9½ × 5-inch rectangles, 4 white 2 × 18½-inch strips, 8 red 2 × 18½-inch strips, 8 white 2 × 9½-inch strips, 4 red 2 × 9½-inch strips.

5 Sew together a white, red, and white 2 × 9½-inch strip. Make 4. Sew each set to the right side of a blue 9½ × 5-inch rectangle (piece A). Sew together a red, white, and red 2 × 18½-inch strip. Make 4. Sew each block to bottom of piece A to create a flag. Sew buttons to blue section of flag. Sew flags around center stars block.

6 For accent border: Cut 4 black 1½-inch strips selvage to selvage. Measure through center vertically of flags block and cut 2 strips this measurement. Sew strips to sides of flags block. Measure through center horizontally and cut 2 strips this measurement. Sew strips to top and bottom of block.

7 For bear paws corners: Cut 20 white 2½-inch squares, 12 white 2⅞-inch squares (cut in half diagonally), 16 white 4½-inch squares, 4 white 4⅞-inch squares (cut in half diagonally), 4 white 9 × 12-inch rectangles, 4 blue 9 × 12-inch rectangles.

8 To make speedy triangles: place a white and blue 9 × 12-inch rectangle right sides together. Draw a grid on rectangle of twelve 2⅞-inch squares. Draw a diagonal line through each corner of every square. Sew ¼ inch away from diagonal line, on both sides of line. Cut on all drawn lines (see diagram below). Repeat with remaining rectangles.

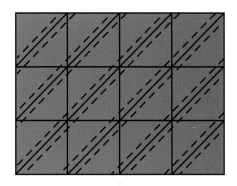

9 Assemble 12 bear paw sets according to diagram A. Assemble 8 bear paw sets according to diagram B. Assemble 4 bear paw sets according to diagram C.

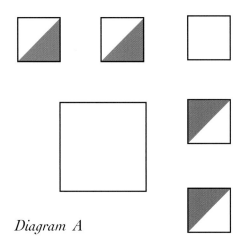

Diagram A

112

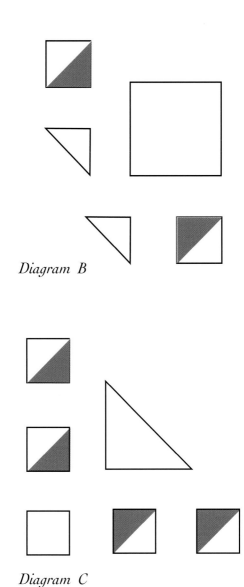

Diagram B

Diagram C

10 Assemble 4 corners according to finished photo. When joining, right sides are even. Add corners onto center flags block. Put opposite corners on first (top and bottom) and then the remaining 2 corners.

11 Cut backing and batting 2 inches larger than quilt face. Place quilt face on top of backing and batting. Pin baste with 1-inch safety pins. Mark quilting design with washable marking pencil. Starting in center, quilt with small even stitches. Trim batting and backing even with quilt face.

12 For binding: Cut six 2½-inch-wide strips width of fabric. Join all strips end to end. Fold in half lengthwise, wrong sides together and press. Measuring through center of quilt lengthwise, cut 2 strips this length. On front side of quilt, with raw edges even, stitch 1 strip to each side. After stitching, fold the binding over the seam allowance to the back. Hand stitch to back along the seam line. Next measure through the center (widthwise), and add 1 inch to this measurement. Cut 2 strips this length. On each end, fold in ½ inch and press. The ½ inch folded in will give your binding a clean finished edge. With wrong sides together press strips in half and follow same procedure as for side binding strips.

Hickory Beef Kabobs

♥

2 ears fresh corn, shucked and
    cleaned
1 pound boneless beef top
    sirloin or tenderloin steak,
    cut into 1¼-inch pieces
1 red or green bell pepper, cut
    into 1-inch squares
1 small red onion, cut into
    ½-inch wedges
½ cup beer or nonalcoholic beer
½ cup chili sauce

1 teaspoon dry mustard
2 cloves garlic, minced
1½ cups hickory chips
4 metal skewers (12 inches
    long)
3 cups hot cooked white rice
¼ cup chopped fresh parsley
    Fresh parsley sprigs and plum
    tomatoes for garnish

1 Place corn on cutting board. Cut crosswise with chef's knife into 1-inch pieces. Place beef, bell pepper, onion, and corn in large resealable plastic food storage bag. Combine beer, chili sauce, mustard, and garlic in small bowl; pour over beef and vegetables. Seal bag tightly, turning to coat. Marinate in refrigerator at least 1 hour or up to 8 hours, turning occasionally.

2 Prepare barbecue grill for direct cooking. Meanwhile, cover hickory chips with cold water; soak 20 minutes.

3 Drain beef and vegetables; reserve marinade. Thread beef and vegetables onto skewers. Brush with reserved marinade.

4 Drain hickory chips; sprinkle over coals. Place kabobs on grill. Grill covered, over medium-hot coals 5 minutes. Brush with reserved marinade; turn and brush again. Discard remaining marinade. Continue to grill, covered, 5 to 7 minutes or until desired doneness is reached.

5 Combine rice and chopped parsley; serve kabobs over rice mixture. Garnish, if desired.

Makes 4 servings

Berry Cobbler

1 Preheat oven to 375°F. Combine berries, ⅓ cup sugar, and cornstarch in bowl; toss lightly to coat. Spoon into 1½-quart baking dish.

2 Combine flour, 1 tablespoon sugar, baking powder, and salt in medium bowl. Add milk and butter; mix just until dry ingredients are moistened.

3 Drop 6 heaping tablespoons of batter evenly over berries; sprinkle with nutmeg. Bake 25 minutes or until topping is golden brown and fruit is bubbly. Cool on wire rack. Serve warm or at room temperature.

Makes 6 servings
*One (16-ounce) bag frozen raspberries and one (16-ounce) bag frozen blueberries or strawberries may be substituted for fresh berries. Thaw berries, reserving juices. Increase cornstarch to 3 tablespoons.

1 pint fresh raspberries
   (2½ cups)*
1 pint fresh blueberries or
   strawberries, sliced
   (2½ cups)*
⅓ cup sugar
2 tablespoons cornstarch
1 cup all-purpose flour

1 tablespoon sugar
1½ teaspoons baking powder
¼ teaspoon salt
½ cup milk
⅓ cup butter or margarine,
   melted
¼ teaspoon ground nutmeg

Watermelon Tote

T hat sweet symbol of summer — the watermelon! Make this fun tote to carry along to all your summer doings. But don't be surprised if someone wants your "recipe" to make this scrumptious bag. ♥

Summer afternoon — summer afternoon; to me those have always been the two most beautiful words in the English language.

Henry James as quoted by Edith Wharton,
A Backward Glance

WHAT YOU'LL NEED

Tracing paper, pencil

½ yard red cotton fabric

¼ yard fusible fleece

⅓ yard green cotton fabric

Scissors

Iron, ironing board

Pins

Sewing machine

12-inch red zipper

Sewing needle

Thread to match red and green fabrics

2 green buttons, ¾ inch each

Black thread

14 seed-shaped black buttons

1 Trace patterns. From red fabric cut out 4 melon sides; from fusible fleece cut out 2 melon sides and 1 rind; from green fabric cut out 2 rinds. Fuse fleece sides to wrong sides of red melon sides. Pin a melon side without fleece to one with fleece, right sides together, and sew around shape, leaving an opening to turn. Trim fleece from seam allowance, clip curves, and turn right side out. Press. Repeat for other melon side. Hand sew openings closed.

2 Machine sew a heavy zigzag (bartack) over zipper teeth ¾ inch in from closed end to shorten zipper. Sew zipper to straight edges of each melon side, beginning and ending ¼ inch from edges of melon sides and allowing zipper teeth to show. Hand sew melon sides together along straight edge beyond zipper opening.

3 Fuse rind fleece to a green rind. Pin other rind to piece, right sides together, and sew, leaving an opening to turn. Trim fleece from seam allowance, clip curves, and turn right side out. Press. Hand sew opening closed.

4 Matching dots on sides to ones on rind, pin melon sides to rind ¼ inch in from rind edges. Tuck zipper ends out of way of seam. With red thread in needle and green thread in bobbin, sew melon sides to rind.

STEP 2

STEP 3

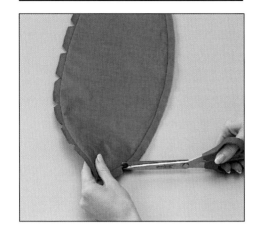

STEP 4

STEP 5

5 Cut 3 × 36-inch piece of green fabric. Fold in half the long way, right sides together. With ¼-inch seam allowance, sew along tube (leave end open for turning). Turn right side out. Press. Sew turning opening closed. Sew to rind using a green button at each end.

6 Using black thread, randomly sew black buttons on melon sides for seeds.

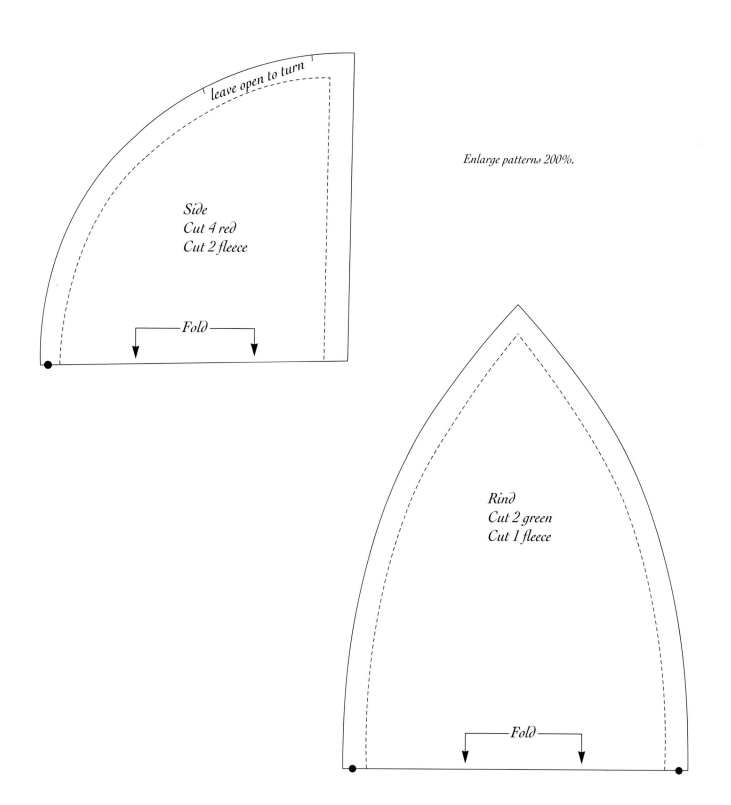

Side
Cut 4 red
Cut 2 fleece

leave open to turn

— *Fold* —

Enlarge patterns 200%.

Rind
Cut 2 green
Cut 1 fleece

— *Fold* —

119

Chicken-Barley Soup

1½ pounds chicken thighs
2 medium ribs celery, sliced
2 medium carrots, peeled, thinly
    sliced
1 small leek, sliced
6 cups cold water
1½ teaspoons salt
½ teaspoon dried marjoram
    leaves, crushed
¼ teaspoon ground black pepper
¼ teaspoon dried summer savory
    leaves, crushed
1 Herb Bouquet*
¼ small red bell pepper
⅓ cup quick-cooking barley
3 cups fresh spinach (loosely
    packed), chopped
    Salt and ground black pepper
      to taste
    Celery leaves for garnish

1 Rinse chicken thighs; remove and discard skin. Place chicken in 5-quart Dutch oven.

2 Add celery, carrots, leek, water, salt, marjoram, black pepper, savory, and Herb Bouquet to Dutch oven. Bring to a boil over high heat. Reduce heat to medium-low; simmer, uncovered, 45 minutes or until chicken is tender.

3 Rinse bell pepper under cold running water. To seed pepper, stand pepper on end on cutting board. Cut off sides in 3 to 4 lengthwise slices with utility knife. (Cut close to, but not through, stem.) Discard stem and seeds. Scrape out any remaining seeds. Rinse inside of pepper under cold running water. Cut into 1-inch-long narrow strips.

4 Remove chicken from soup and let cool slightly. Remove Herb Bouquet; discard. Remove foam and fat from soup by using a large spoon and skimming off as much fat as possible. (Or, refrigerate soup several hours and remove fat that rises to surface. Refrigerate chicken if chilling soup to remove fat.)

5 Add barley to soup. Bring to a boil over high heat. Reduce heat to medium-low; simmer, uncovered, 10 minutes or until barley is almost tender.

6 Meanwhile, remove chicken meat from bones; discard bones. Cut chicken into bite-size pieces.

7 Stir chicken, spinach, and bell pepper into soup. Simmer 5 minutes or until spinach is wilted, chicken is heated, and bell pepper is tender. Season with additional salt and black pepper to taste. Ladle into bowls. Garnish, if desired.

Makes 6 servings
*A herb bouquet is a bundle of seasoning ingredients that are either tied with string or wrapped in cheesecloth.

Calico Bell Pepper Muffins

♥

¼ cup each finely chopped red, yellow, and green bell peppers
¼ cup butter or margarine
2 cups all-purpose flour
2 tablespoons sugar
1 tablespoon baking powder
¾ teaspoon salt
½ teaspoon dried basil leaves
1 cup milk
2 eggs

1 Preheat oven to 400°F. Grease or paper-line 12 (2½-inch) muffin cups. In small skillet, over medium-high heat, cook peppers in butter until color is bright and pepper is tender crisp—about 3 minutes. Set aside.

2 In large bowl, combine flour, sugar, baking powder, salt, and basil. In small bowl, combine milk and eggs until blended. Add milk mixture and peppers with drippings to flour mixture. Stir just until moistened. Spoon into muffin cups. Bake 15 minutes or until golden and wooden pick inserted in center comes out clean. Remove from pan.

Makes 12 muffins

This is a rather moist batter, but results in a light and tender muffin, which is especially good with chicken. ♥

Honey-Orange
Tea Sampler

♥

T his homey sampler is a great addition to any kitchen, and the lemon bars are so tasty. ♥

WHAT YOU'LL NEED

6 × 17-inch piece champagne linen

Embroidery floss (see color key)

Embroidery needle

Frame with 2½ × 10¾-inch opening

Each stitch will be made over 2 threads of linen. Stitch with 2 strands of floss and backstitch with 1 strand. Pattern overlays at arrows.

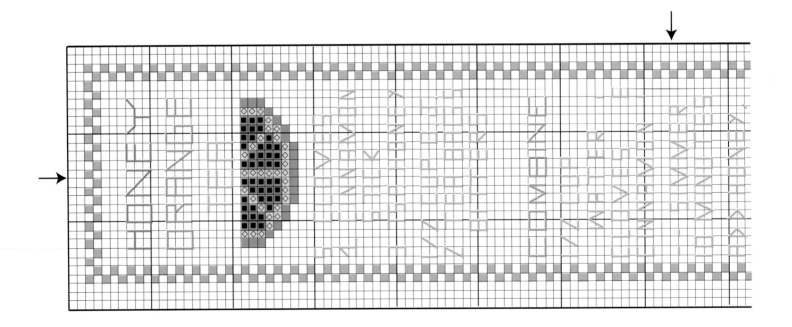

Color		DMC
■	Black	310
	Green	367
	Yellow	725
◇	Cream	Ecru
▫	Light tan	676
	Dark tan	435
●	Brown	433
	Light orange	722
■	Dark orange	946

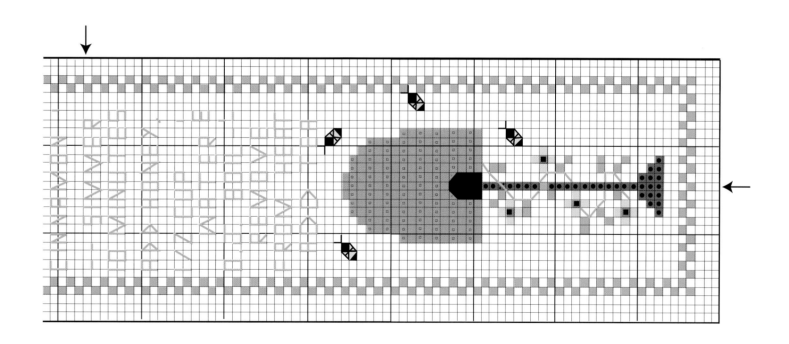

125

Luscious Lemon Bars

♥

2 lemons
2 cups all-purpose flour
1 cup butter
½ cup powdered sugar
¼ teaspoon salt
1 cup granulated sugar
3 large eggs
⅓ cup fresh lemon juice
　Sifted powdered sugar

1 Finely grate colored portion of lemon peel using bell grater or hand-held grater. Measure 4 teaspoons lemon peel; set aside.

2 Preheat oven to 350°F. Grease 13 × 9-inch baking pan; set aside. Place 1 teaspoon lemon peel, flour, butter, powdered sugar, and salt in food processor. Process until mixture forms coarse crumbs.

3 Press mixture evenly into prepared 13 × 9-inch baking pan. Bake 18 to 20 minutes or until golden brown.

4 Beat remaining 3 teaspoons lemon peel, granulated sugar, eggs, and lemon juice in medium bowl with electric mixer. Beat at medium speed until well blended.

5 Pour mixture evenly over warm crust. Return to oven; bake 18 to 20 minutes or until center is set and edges are golden brown. Remove pan to wire rack; cool completely.

6 Dust with sifted powdered sugar; cut into 2 × 1½-inch bars.

7 Store tightly covered at room temperature. Do not freeze.

Makes 3 dozen bars

I believe in the forest, and in the meadow, and in the night in which the corn grows.

Henry David Thoreau
"Walking"

Country Barn Tissue Cover

♥

Camouflage a boutique tissue box with a replica of a country barn! The open barn doors reveal a contented, hay-munching cow. This is a fun, easy plastic canvas project.♥

WHAT YOU'LL NEED

12 × 18-inch ultrastiff plastic canvas

Scissors

#18 tapestry needle

Plastic canvas yarn (see color key)

6-strand embroidery floss: gray, black

Raffia

Monofilament thread

Colors
- ■ Black
- ▨ Gray
- ■ Red
- □ Eggshell
- ☐ Natural
- ▨ Denim
- ▨ Pink

1 Carefully cut pieces from plastic canvas according to charts. For barn back, use pattern for front but without cutouts. Use 1 strand yarn to work all continental, slanting gobelin, overcast, and longstitches. Use 6 strands of floss to work French knots on cow: gray for nostrils, black for eyes. For barn back, work as front but without cutouts for windows and doors.

2 Use eggshell to join door and window inserts to front openings. With eggshell, join doors and windows through empty holes in inserts. Stitch randomly with raffia to fill empty holes in hayloft. Work loops across bottom row. Cut loops and trim unevenly. Insert small piece of raffia through cow's mouth where indicated on chart by small dashes.

3 Use eggshell to join barn sides at corners. Use red to overcast bottom and top edges of barn.

4 Use denim to join roof pieces and to overcast opening and edges. Use monofilament thread to tack roof on where indicated on chart by Xs.

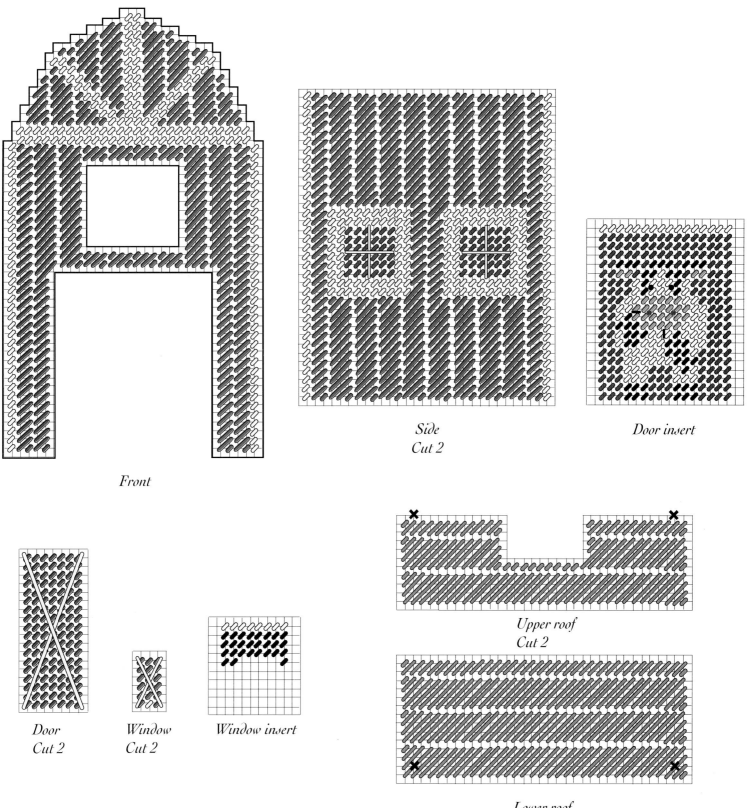

Front

Side
Cut 2

Door insert

Door
Cut 2

Window
Cut 2

Window insert

Upper roof
Cut 2

Lower roof
Cut 2

129

Southern Fried Catfish with Hush Puppies

♥

There is nothing more down-home country than catfish and hush puppies. ♥

Hush Puppy Batter (recipe
    follows)
4 catfish fillets (about 1½
    pounds)
½ cup yellow cornmeal
3 tablespoons all-purpose flour
1½ teaspoons salt
¼ teaspoon ground red pepper
    Vegetable oil for frying
    Fresh parsley sprigs for
    garnish

1 Prepare Hush Puppy Batter; set aside.

2 Rinse catfish and pat dry with paper towels.

3 Combine cornmeal, flour, salt, and red pepper in shallow dish. Dip fish in cornmeal mixture.

4 Heat 1 inch of oil in large, heavy saucepan over medium heat until a fresh bread cube placed in oil browns in 45 seconds (about 365°F).

5 Fry fish, a few pieces at a time, 4 to 5 minutes or until golden brown and fish flakes easily when tested with fork. Adjust heat to maintain temperature. (Allow temperature of oil to return to 365°F between each batch.) Drain fish on paper towels.

6 To make Hush Puppies, place 1 tablespoon of batter into hot oil. Fry a few pieces at a time, 2 minutes or until golden brown. Garnish, if desired.

Makes 4 servings

HUSH PUPPY BATTER
1½ cups yellow cornmeal
½ cup all-purpose flour
2 teaspoons baking powder
½ teaspoon salt
1 egg
1 cup milk
1 small onion, minced

Combine cornmeal, flour, baking powder, and salt in medium bowl. Add egg, milk, and onion. Stir until well combined. Allow batter to stand 5 to 10 minutes before frying.

Makes about 24 hush puppies

Best Ever Apple Pie

♥

Nothing compares to the pleasure of a homemade apple pie. What a great way to finish off that delicious summer barbeque. ♥

2⅓ cups all-purpose flour, divided
  ¾ cup plus 1 tablespoon sugar, divided
  ½ teaspoon baking powder
  ½ teaspoon salt
  ¾ cup cold unsalted butter
  4 to 5 tablespoons ice water
  1 egg white
  7 medium apples such as Jonathan, Macintosh, or Granny Smith, peeled, cored, sliced
  1 tablespoon lemon juice
1¼ teaspoons ground cinnamon
  3 tablespoons unsalted butter, cut into small pieces
  1 egg yolk
  1 tablespoon sour cream

1 Combine 2 cups flour, 1 tablespoon sugar, baking powder, and salt in large bowl until well blended. Cut in butter using pastry blender or 2 knives until mixture resembles coarse crumbs.

2 Add water, 1 tablespoon at a time, to flour mixture. Toss with fork until mixture holds together. Form dough into 2 (6-inch) discs. Wrap discs in plastic wrap; refrigerate 30 minutes or until firm.

3 Working with 1 disc at a time, unwrap dough and place on lightly floured surface. Roll out dough in short strokes, starting in the middle of disc and rolling out towards edge with lightly floured rolling pin.

4 Rotate dough ¼ turn to the right. Sprinkle more flour under dough and on rolling pin as necessary to prevent sticking. Roll out dough into 12-inch circle, ⅛ inch thick.

5 Place rolling pin on one side of dough. Gently roll dough over rolling pin once. Carefully lift rolling pin and dough, unrolling dough over 9-inch glass pie plate.

6 Ease dough into pie plate with fingertips. Do not stretch dough. Trim dough leaving ½-inch overhang; brush with egg white. Set aside.

7 Preheat oven to 450°F. Place apple slices in large bowl; sprinkle with lemon juice. Combine remaining ⅓ cup flour, ¾ cup sugar, and cinnamon in small bowl with wooden spoon until

well blended. Add to apple mixture; toss to coat apples evenly. Spoon filling into prepared pie crust; place butter on top of filling.

8 Moisten edge of dough with water. Roll out remaining disc as described in Steps 3 to 5. Place on top of filled pie as described in Step 6. Trim dough leaving ½-inch overhang.

9 To flute, press dough between thumb and forefinger to make stand-up edge. Cut slits in dough at ½-inch intervals around edge to form flaps.

10 Press 1 flap in toward center of pie and the next out toward rim of pie plate. Continue alternating in and out around edge of pie. Cut 4 small slits in top of dough with paring knife to allow steam to escape.

11 Combine egg yolk and sour cream in small bowl until well blended. Cover; refrigerate until ready to use.

12 Bake 10 minutes; reduce oven temperature to 375°F. Bake 35 minutes. Brush egg yolk mixture evenly on pie crust with pastry brush. Bake 20 to 25 minutes or until crust is deep golden brown.

13 Cool pie completely in pie plate on wire rack. Store loosely covered at room temperature 1 day or refrigerate up to 4 days.

Makes 1 (9-inch) pie

And then there crept
A little noiseless noise among the
leaves,
Born of the very sigh that silences
heaves.

John Keats
"I Stood Tiptoe"

Welcome Friends
Hanging Hoop

Tracing paper, pencil

Scissors

Water-erasable marker

9 × 12-inch felt pieces: denim blue, antique white, ½ piece cranberry, ½ piece peach

#20 chenille needle

6-strand cotton embroidery floss: blue (DMC 311), red (DMC 221), ecru

Pins

11 white sew-through buttons, ⅜ inch each

6-inch wooden embroidery hoop

Craft glue

Raffia

2 small magnets

Stitch a heartfelt welcome to greet all who enter your home or kitchen. ♥

1 Trace entire pattern onto tracing paper to make guide for placing pieces. Also trace each pattern piece separately and cut out to make templates (or make 6 photocopies of pattern). Mark lettering with dots on scalloped circle template. Use marker to trace around templates onto felt. From denim felt cut out 2 small hearts, 1 scalloped circle; from antique white felt cut out 1 scalloped circle, 1 outer heart; from cranberry felt cut out 1 outer teapot, 1 inner heart; from peach felt cut out 1 inner teapot.

2 Use needle to poke holes through template where dots appear in letters. Transfer lettering placement to antique white scalloped circle by marking dots through holes in template. Use floss to work lettering by backstitching between dots. Use 6 strands floss for all stitching.

3 Pin hearts on peach teapot according to pattern. Use blue floss to straight stitch cranberry and antique hearts as one. Cross-stitch buttons through center of hearts. Use ecru floss to straight stitch denim hearts in place. Cross-stitch button in center of each with red floss.

4 Pin peach teapot to cranberry. Use red floss to backstitch horizontal lines at base and lid on peach teapot, through both layers. Use ecru floss to work vertical straight stitches at base and lid of peach teapot and blanket stitch peach teapot to cranberry teapot. Pin teapots to antique white scalloped circle. Use blue floss to blanket stitch teapots in place. Remove any unwanted marker with cold water.

5 Center antique white scalloped circle over smaller hoop. With closure at top, position larger hoop and press in place. Run a bead of glue along hoop edge on back. Position hooped piece on denim scalloped circle so that scallops offset antique white ones. Place heavy book on hoop until glue dries.

6 Use red floss to blanket stitch antique white scalloped edge to denim. Cross-stitch remaining buttons in every other scallop with red floss. Tie raffia bow around hoop closure. Glue magnets to back of piece.

The poetry of earth is never dead.

John Keats
"On the Grasshopper and the Cricket"

136

Herb Rack

♥

WHAT YOU'LL NEED

Large wood herb rack, with 5 hole openings

3 ounces dried lavender

3 ounces dried oregano

3 ounces preserved mountain mint

3 ounces dried white larkspur

20 stems dried peach roses

10 strands raffia

Wire cutters

Add a fresh garden fragrance to your home and have your culinary herbs near at hand with this eye-catching aromatic herb and decorative flower rack. ♥

STEP 1

1 Cut bundles of dried herbs and flowers 15 to 22 inches long.

STEP 2

2 Insert bundles through hole openings of rack. Remove any additional leaves on the bottom of the stems for easier insertion into opening.

STEP 3

3 Tie each bundle with strands of raffia.

TIP
Dry your favorite summer garden herbs for display and cooking, such as dill, rosemary, oregano, mint, parsley, basil, and sage.

He drove past grey-shingled farm-houses in orchards, past hayfields and groves of oak, past villages with white steeples rising sharply into the fading sky.

Edith Wharton
The Age of Innocence

AUTUMN

CRISP RED AND YELLOW
LEAVES CRUNCHING
UNDERFOOT, THE SHARP
BITE OF THE MORNING
AIR, COMFY HEAVY
WOOLEN SWEATERS—
HOW THIS TIME OF YEAR
ENCHANTS US!

Henrietta Witch

♥

Crown'd with the sickle, and the wheaten sheaf,
While Autumn, nodding o'er the yellow plain,
Comes jovial on.

James Thompson
The Seasons "Autumn"

Henrietta is a nice witch, even though she is ready to fly away to her Halloween haunts at any minute! She is sure to delight all your little ghosts and goblins. ♥

Up from the meadows rich with corn,
Clear in the cool September morn.

John Greenleaf Whittier
"Barbara Frietchie" [1864]

¼ yard unbleached muslin

1 package tan dye

Plastic or cardboard

Scissors

Water-erasable marker, fabric marking pencil

Sewing machine

Cream thread

Pins

10 ounces polyester fiberfill

¼ yard each brown and black check, brown plaid, black fabrics

2 black seed beads

10 inches red embroidery floss

Blusher

1 ounce wool roving for hair

White craft glue

½ yard black ribbon, ⅛ inch wide

9-inch wooden meat skewer

1½ × 4-inch piece gold-brown fabric

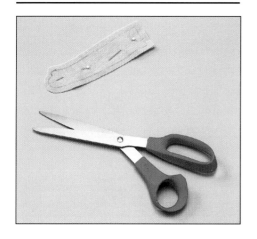

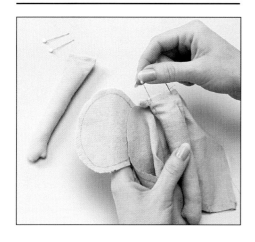

3 With muslin folded (9 × 22-inches), trace arms and head-body, leaving ½ inch between pieces. Traced lines are seam lines. Cut around all pieces ¼ inch away from seam lines.

4 Stitch around arms, leaving top open. Clip curves and turn right side out. Stuff to 1 inch below top. Baste top closed.

5 Stitch from A to B around head. Pin arms in place at sides. Stitch sides catching arms in seams. Clip curves and turn right side out.

6 Cut 2½ × 15-inch piece from black, cut 9 × 15-inch piece from muslin. Stitch pieces together along 15-inch side and press seam toward black fabric. On wrong side of doubled fabric, trace leg-shoe twice, lining up seam line with seam. (Remember to leave ½ inch between pieces.) Cut out leg-shoe ¼ inch from traced lines.

1 Wash and dry muslin. Do not use fabric softener. Following manufacturer's directions, dye muslin in sink.

2 Trace and cut all pattern pieces on cardboard or plastic. Leg-shoe is one piece and seam line is marked.

7 Stitch around leg-shoe on traced lines, leaving top open. Clip curves and turn right side out. Stuff to 1½ inches below top. Place seams side by side and baste across the top.

8 Stitch legs to front body at opening, making sure feet are forward. Stuff head and body and stitch opening closed.

9 Pinch face together to form nose and take 2 stitches through pinched fabric and fiberfill. Stitch on seed beads for eyes. With red floss embroider mouth. Using finger put blush on cheeks.

10 Trace and cut out dress and sleeves from check fabric, vest from plaid, and hat from black.

11 Stitch dress at shoulder seams, and stitch sleeves to dress. Fringe bottom of sleeves by cutting slits 1 inch deep and ¼ inch apart. Stitch sleeve and side seams. Fringe bottom of dress in the same manner as sleeves. Hem neck opening. Place dress on doll and gather at neck and sleeves above fringe.

12 Cut front vest at fold line. Hem vest armholes, neck, front, and bottom. Stitch shoulder seams. Place vest on doll.

STEP 8

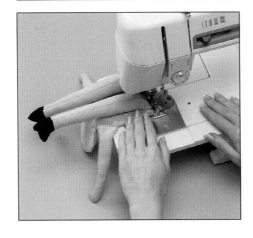

STEP 11

STEP 13

STEP 14

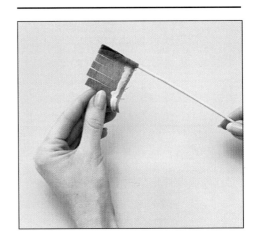

13 Using craft glue, glue wool roving on doll to form hair. Use fingers to lightly comb hair. Stitch back seam on hat and turn right side out. Turn brim of hat up in front and glue in place. Glue hat on doll's head. Tie black ribbon into a bow and glue to front neck of dress.

14 Fringe gold-brown fabric in same manner as sleeves. Glue to end of meat skewer. Roll fabric around bottom of skewer, glue as you roll to form broom. Stitch broom to hands at thumbs.

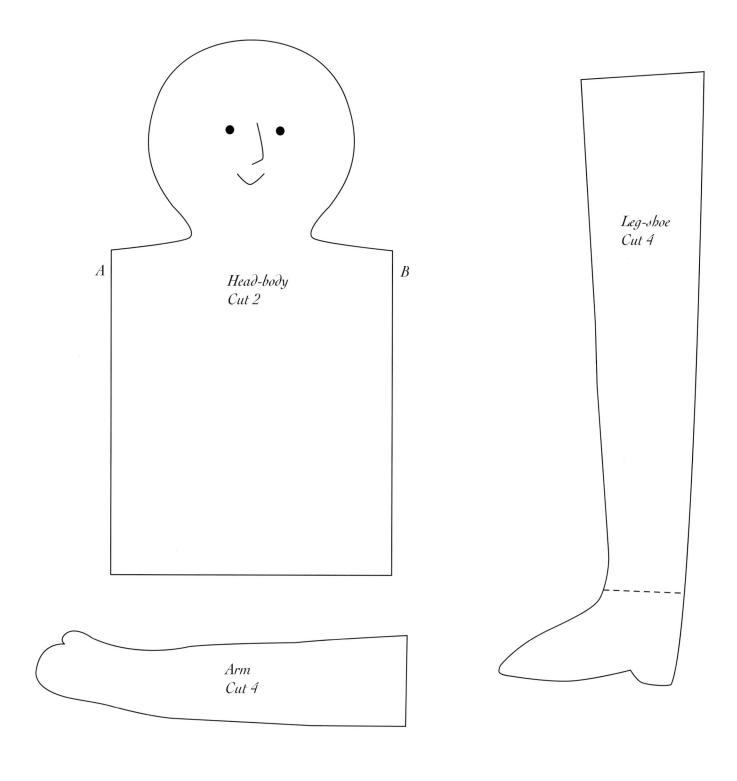

Head-body
Cut 2

A

B

Arm
Cut 4

Leg-shoe
Cut 4

Patterns are 100%.

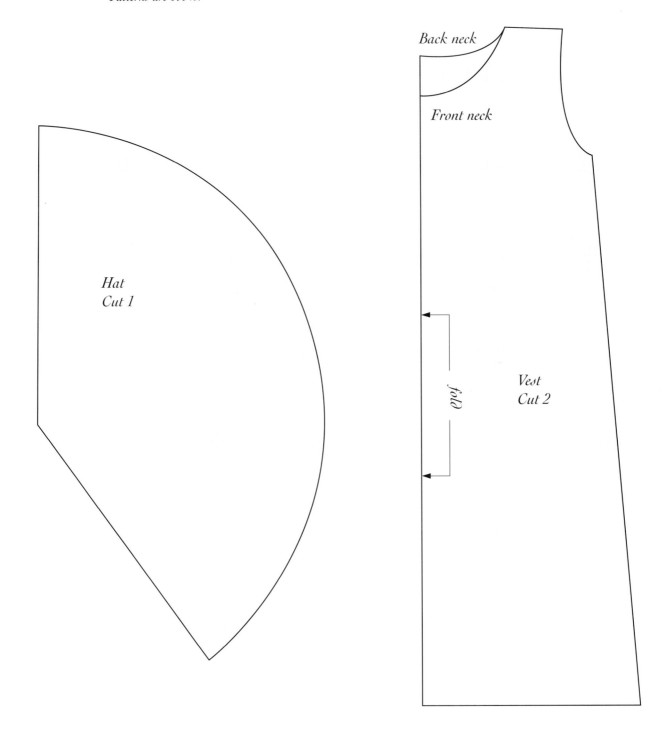

Back neck

Front neck

Hat
Cut 1

fold

Vest
Cut 2

Patterns are 100%.

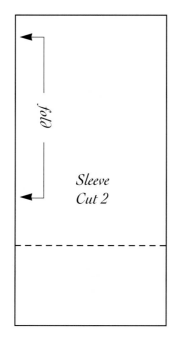

fold

Sleeve
Cut 2

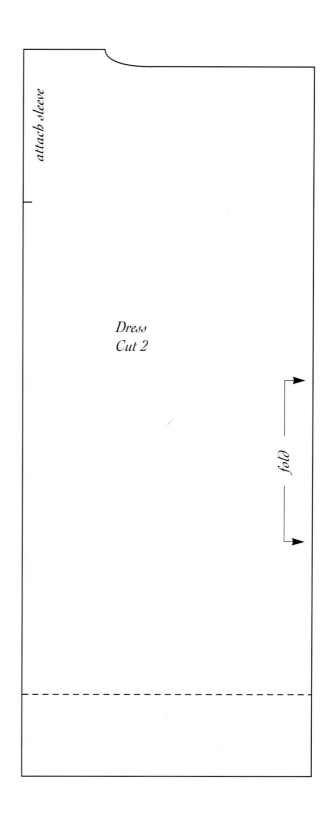

attach sleeve

Dress
Cut 2

fold

Potato & Cheddar Soup

♥

T hick and rich, this scrumptious soup is perfect to chase away the autumn chill. ♥

2 cups water
2 cups red potatoes, peeled and
   cut into cubes
3 tablespoons butter or
   margarine
1 small onion, finely chopped
3 tablespoons all-purpose flour
   Red and black pepper to taste
3 cups milk
½ teaspoon sugar
1 cup shredded Cheddar cheese
1 cup cubed cooked ham

1 Bring water to a boil in large saucepan. Add potatoes and cook until tender. Drain, reserving liquid. Measure 1 cup, adding water if necessary.

2 Melt butter in saucepan over medium heat. Add onion; cook and stir until tender but not brown. Add flour; season with red and black pepper. Cook 3 to 4 minutes.

3 Gradually add potatoes, reserved liquid, milk, and sugar to onion mixture; stir well. Add cheese and ham. Simmer over low heat 30 minutes, stirring frequently.

Makes 12 servings

Whole Wheat Popovers

♥

2 eggs
1 cup milk
2 tablespoons butter or
    margarine, melted
½ cup all-purpose flour
½ cup whole wheat flour
¼ teaspoon salt

1 Position rack in lower third of oven. Preheat oven to 450°F. Grease 6 (6-ounce) custard cups. Set custard cups in jelly-roll pan for easier handling; set aside.

2 Beat eggs in large bowl with electric mixer at low speed 1 minute. Beat in milk and butter until blended. Beat in flours and salt until batter is smooth. Pour evenly into prepared custard cups.

3 Bake 20 minutes. Reduce oven temperature to 350°F. Bake 15 minutes more; quickly make small slit in top of each popover to let out steam. Bake 5 to 10 minutes more or until browned. Remove from cups. Cool on wire rack 10 minutes. Serve warm or cool completely.

Makes 6 popovers

This rather simple recipe looks deceptively difficult to make. Your family will think you slaved for hours. ♥

Burlap Apple Bag

♥

This apple bag is perfect for a casual table centerpiece filled with apples. Or fill the bag with delicious Apple Butter Spice Muffins! ♥

WHAT YOU'LL NEED

Burlap cross-stitch bag

Embroidery floss (see color key)

Embroidery needle

Do all stitching with 6 strands of floss. Follow design all the way around the bag, repeating design as necessary.

Colors		DMC
	Light green	367
	Dark green	319
	Cream	746
	Tan	677
	Light red	221
	Medium red	204
	Dark red	349
	Blue	312

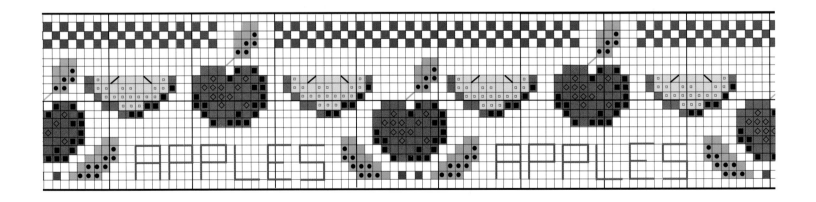

Apple Butter Spice Muffins

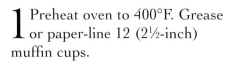

½ cup pecans or walnuts
½ cup sugar
1 teaspoon ground cinnamon
¼ teaspoon ground nutmeg
⅛ teaspoon ground allspice
2 cups all-purpose flour
2 teaspoons baking powder
¼ teaspoon salt
1 cup milk
¼ cup vegetable oil
1 egg
¼ cup apple butter

1 Preheat oven to 400°F. Grease or paper-line 12 (2½-inch) muffin cups.

2 Place pecans on cutting board; chop with chef's knife. Combine sugar, cinnamon, nutmeg, and allspice in large bowl. Toss 2 tablespoons sugar mixture with pecans in small bowl; set aside. Add flour, baking powder, and salt to remaining sugar mixture.

3 Combine milk, oil, and egg in medium bowl. Stir into flour mixture just until moistened.

4 Spoon 1 tablespoon batter into each prepared muffin cup. Spoon 1 teaspoon apple butter into each cup. Spoon remaining batter over apple butter. Sprinkle reserved sugar-nut mixture over each muffin.

5 Bake 20 to 25 minutes or until golden brown and wooden toothpick inserted in center comes out clean. Immediately remove from pan; cool on wire rack 10 minutes. Serve warm or cold.

Makes 12 muffins

Clear cascades!

Into the waves scatter

Blue pine needles.

Matsuo Bashō
"The Narrow Road of Oku"

Country Scents Quilt

What better way to bring the country into your kitchen than with chickens, apple pie, jam, and tea? ♥

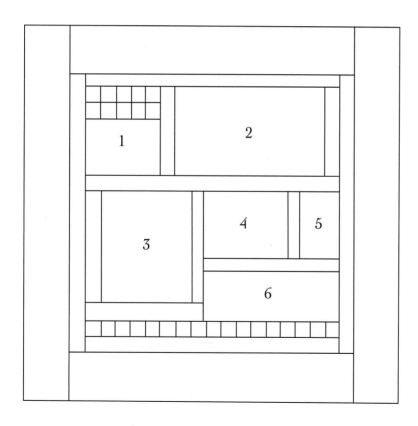

Rotary cutter, self-healing mat, see-through ruler

½ yard background fabric

⅜ yard lattice and binding fabric

Scraps of 1½-inch pieces of checkerboard and multicolor stripes (22 pieces)

¼ yard accent border

⅜ yard outside border

¾ yard backing fabric

27-inch piece batting

Safety pins

Iron, ironing board

⅜ yard fusible webbing

5-inch fabric piece for chicken

9-inch fabric piece for pie

6-inch fabric piece for teapot

5-inch fabric piece for basket

3-inch fabric piece for each apple

3-inch fabric piece for jam jar

Scraps of reds, blacks, browns

Washable marking pencil

Quilting needle, thread

1 All seam allowances are ¼ inch. Always iron seams to darkest fabric. There are 6 sections of quilt: Section 1 has 1 chicken, section 2 has pie, section 3 has teapot, section 4 has apple basket, section 5 has jam jar, section 6 has 2 chickens. Cut and sew 1 section at a time. Measurements are listed widths first, then heights.

2 For section 1: Cut 5½ × 4-inch background piece, 1½ × 6-inch lattice piece, five 1½-inch dark checkerboard squares, five 1½-inch light checkerboard squares. Sew 5 alternating light to dark checkerboard squares together right to left. Sew 5 alternating dark to light checkerboard squares together right to left. Sew strips on top of each other with darker outside squares on top. Sew checkerboard to top of 5½ × 4-inch background piece. Sew 1½ × 6-inch lattice piece to right side of checkerboard/background block.

3 For section 2: Cut 10½ × 6-inch background piece, 1½ × 6-inch lattice piece, 17½ × 1½-inch lattice piece. Sew 10½ × 6-inch background piece to right side of block from Step 2. Sew 1½ × 6-inch lattice piece to right of 10½ × 6-inch background piece. Sew 17½ × 1½-inch lattice piece to bottom of complete sections 1 and 2.

4 For section 3: Cut 6½ × 7½-inch background piece, 1¼ × 7½-inch lattice piece, 1½ × 7½-

inch lattice piece, 8¼ × 1¾-inch lattice piece. Sew 1¼ × 7½-inch lattice piece to the right side of the background piece and the 1½ × 7½-inch piece to the left side. Sew 8¼ × 1¾-inch lattice piece to bottom of block.

5 For section 4: Cut 6¼ × 4¾-inch background piece, 1¼ × 4¾-inch lattice piece. Sew lattice piece to right side of background piece.

6 For section 5: Cut 3¼ × 4¾-inch background piece, 9¾ × 1¼-inch lattice piece. Sew background piece to right of block created in Step 5. Sew lattice piece cut in this Step to bottom of section 4 and 5 (with lattice piece between).

7 For section 6: Cut 9¾ × 3¾-inch background piece. Sew background piece to bottom of block created in Step 6. Sew this block to the right of section 3. Sew top and bottom blocks together.

8 Cut seventeen 1½-inch squares from multicolor scraps. Sew squares together to form strip. Sew this strip to bottom of already created block.

9 For accent border: From accent border fabric cut two 1½ × 17½-inch strips and two 18¼ × 1½-inch strips. Sew 1½ × 17½-inch strips to top and bottom of block. Sew 18¼ × 1½-inch strips to right and left sides of block.

10 For outside border: From outside border fabric cut two 19½ × 3½-inch strips and two 3½ × 24¼-inch strips. Sew 19½ × 3½-inch strips to top and bottom of block. Sew 3½ × 24¼-inch strips to right and left sides of block.

11 Cut backing and batting 2 inches larger than quilt face. Place quilt face on top of backing and batting. Pin baste with 1-inch safety pins. Trim batting and backing even with quilt face.

12 For binding: Cut six 2½-inch-wide strips of fabric (selvage to selvage). Join all strips end to end. Fold in half lengthwise, wrong sides together and press. Measuring through center of quilt lengthwise, cut 2 strips this length. On front side of quilt, with raw edges even, stitch 1 strip to each side. After stitching, fold the binding over the seam allowance to the back. Hand stitch to back along the seam line. Next measure through the center (widthwise), and add 1 inch to this measurement. Cut 2 strips this length. On each end, fold in ½ inch and press. The ½-inch fold in will give your binding a clean finished edge. With wrong sides together press strips in half and follow same procedure as for side binding strips.

13 Iron fusible webbing to wrong side of all appliqué fabrics. Trace patterns on paper side of webbing and cut out patterns (patterns are already reversed). If you are hand appliquéing, be sure to cut out patterns ½ inch larger than drawn for seam allowance. Remove paper backing. Lay out pieces on quilt and fuse to quilt. Machine quilt, buttonhole stitch, or pen stitch around pieces. Mark quilting design with washable marking pencil. Starting in center, quilt with small even stitches.

MAL

Enlarge patterns 125%.

Enlarge patterns 125%.

Harvest Pumpkin Cookies

♥

After raking up all those fall leaves, your family will need an extra-special treat. These cookies fill the bill. ♥

2 cups all-purpose flour
1 teaspoon baking powder
1 teaspoon ground cinnamon
½ teaspoon baking soda
½ teaspoon salt
½ teaspoon ground allspice
1 cup butter, softened
1 cup sugar
1 cup canned pumpkin
1 large egg
1 teaspoon vanilla
1 cup chopped pecans
1 cup dried cranberries
    (optional)
  Pecan halves

1 Preheat oven to 375°F.

2 Place flour, baking powder, cinnamon, baking soda, salt, and allspice in medium bowl; stir to combine.

3 Beat butter and sugar in large bowl with electric mixer at medium speed until light and fluffy, scraping down side of bowl once. Beat in pumpkin, egg, and vanilla. Gradually add flour mixture. Beat at low speed until well blended, scraping down side of bowl once. Stir in chopped pecans and, if desired, cranberries, with spoon.

4 Drop heaping tablespoonfuls of dough 2 inches apart onto ungreased cookie sheets. Flatten mounds slightly with back of spoon.

5 Press one pecan half into center of each mound. Bake 10 to 12 minutes or until golden brown.

6 Let cookies stand on cookie sheets 1 minute. Remove cookies with spatula to wire racks; cool completely. Store tightly covered at room temperature or freeze up to 3 months.

Makes about 3 dozen cookies

160

Gingerbread Pear Muffins

♥

1¾ cups all-purpose flour
⅓ cup sugar
2 teaspoons baking powder
¾ teaspoon ground ginger
¼ teaspoon baking soda
¼ teaspoon salt
¼ teaspoon ground cinnamon
1 medium pear
⅓ cup milk
¼ cup vegetable oil
¼ cup light molasses
1 egg

1 Preheat oven to 375°F. Grease or paper-line 12 (2½-inch) muffin cups.

2 Sift flour, sugar, baking powder, ginger, baking soda, salt, and cinnamon into large bowl.

3 Peel pear with vegetable peeler. Cut pear lengthwise into halves, then into quarters with utility knife. Remove core and seeds. Finely chop pear with chef's knife. Chop enough to make 1 cup.

4 Combine milk, oil, molasses, and egg in medium bowl. Stir in pear. Stir milk mixture into flour mixture just until moistened.

5 Spoon evenly into prepared muffin cups, filling ⅔ full. Bake 20 minutes or until wooden toothpick inserted in center comes out clean. Immediately remove from pan; cool on wire rack 10 minutes. Serve warm or cold.

Makes 12 muffins

Halloween Delights

♥

Your favorite kid is going to love this special, sturdy bag for holding all his or her treats! ♥

STEP 2

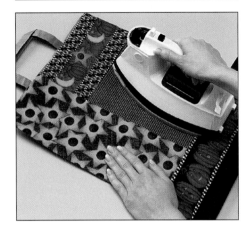

STEP 4

STEP 6

STEP 7

1 Cut two 17 × 12-inch pieces of fusible webbing. From the halloween fabrics cut a 12 × 5-inch piece, 4⅛ × 7-inch piece, 8 × 7-inch piece, 5 × 12-inch piece. Cut 17 × 12-inch piece fabric for bag back.

2 Lay fabric sections for bag front onto a piece of fusible

webbing and fuse according to manufacturer's directions. Adhere back fabric to other piece of fusible webbing. Remove paper backing. Bond to front and back of bag.

3 Iron fusible webbing to black fabric for cutouts. Trace and cut pattern pieces from desired fabrics. Remove paper backing.

4 Arrange cutouts on bag front using picture as guide. Press in place. With permanent marker write "Trick or Treat" on moon.

5 Cover entire bag with vinyl. To determine amount, measure bag beginning at top of bag front, down under bag bottom, and back up to top of bag back, and add 1 inch. Cut measured amount.

6 Center bag bottom on center of paper side of vinyl. Vinyl will be wider than bag, excess will aid in covering bag sides. Mark bag bottom corners on paper backing. Cut vinyl to mark from each edge.

7 Remove paper backing to first set of cuts. Lay bag front onto sticky side of vinyl. Hand press in place. Fold excess vinyl onto sides of bag. Continue to remove paper backing to next set of cuts. Hand press bag bottom in place, leaving excess on sides alone. Remove remaining paper backing, hand press to bag back and fold excess to bag sides. Fold bottom excess up onto bag sides. Fold any excess at top of bag to inside, making cuts at handles for proper fit. Iron according to manufacturer's directions. Cut pieces of vinyl to fit uncovered bag area on sides. Bond using manufacturer's directions.

Enlarge patterns 125%.

Navajo Lamb Stew with Cornmeal Dumplings

♥

2 pounds lean lamb stew meat with bones, cut into 2-inch pieces or 1½ pounds lean boneless lamb, cut into 1½-inch cubes
1 teaspoon salt
½ teaspoon pepper
2½ tablespoons vegetable oil, divided
1 large onion, chopped
1 clove garlic, minced
4 cups water
2 tablespoons tomato paste
2 teaspoons chili powder
1 teaspoon ground coriander
3 small potatoes, cut into 1½-inch chunks
2 large carrots, cut into 1-inch pieces
1 package (10 ounces) frozen whole kernel corn
⅓ cup coarsely chopped celery leaves
Cornmeal Dumplings (recipe follows)
Whole celery leaves for garnish

1 Sprinkle meat with salt and pepper. Heat 2 tablespoons oil in 5-quart Dutch oven over medium-high heat. Add meat a few pieces at a time; cook until browned. Transfer meat to medium bowl.

2 Heat remaining ½ tablespoon oil over medium heat. Add onion and garlic; cook until onion is tender. Stir in water, tomato paste, chili powder, and coriander. Return meat to Dutch oven. Add potatoes, carrots, corn, and chopped celery leaves. Bring to a boil. Cover; reduce heat and simmer 1 hour and 15 minutes or until meat is tender.

3 During last 15 minutes of cooking, prepare Cornmeal Dumplings. Drop dough onto stew to make 6 dumplings. Cover and simmer 18 minutes or until dumplings are firm to the touch and wooden pick inserted in center comes out clean. To serve, spoon stew onto individual plates; serve with dumplings. Garnish with whole celery leaves.

Makes 6 servings

CORNMEAL DUMPLINGS
½ cup yellow cornmeal
½ cup all-purpose flour
1 teaspoon baking powder
¼ teaspoon salt
2½ tablespoons cold butter or margarine
½ cup milk

Combine cornmeal, flour, baking powder, and salt in medium bowl. Cut in butter with fingers, pastry blender, or 2 knives until mixture resembles coarse crumbs. Make a well in center; pour in milk all at once and stir with fork until mixture forms dough.

Denver Spoonbread

♥

This bread combines the tantalizing flavors of tangy bell peppers with cheesy cornbread. ♥

3 tablespoons butter or
    margarine, divided
2 tablespoons freshly grated
    Parmesan cheese
½ cup chopped onion
¼ cup chopped green bell pepper
¼ cup chopped red bell pepper
2½ cups milk
1 cup yellow cornmeal
1 teaspoon salt
1½ cups (6 ounces) shredded
    Cheddar cheese
4 eggs, separated*
    Red and green bell pepper
    strips for garnish

1 Preheat oven to 350°F. Grease 1½-quart souffle dish with 1 tablespoon butter. Sprinkle bottom and side of dish evenly with Parmesan cheese.

2 Melt remaining 2 tablespoons butter in heavy medium saucepan over medium heat. Add onion and green and red bell peppers; cook 5 to 7 minutes or until tender, stirring occasionally. Transfer mixture to small bowl; set aside.

3 Combine milk, cornmeal, and salt in same saucepan. Bring to a boil over high heat. Reduce heat to medium; cook and stir 5 minutes or until mixture thickens. Remove from heat.

4 Stir in Cheddar cheese with wooden spoon until cheese is melted. Stir in onion mixture.

5 Beat egg whites in clean large bowl using clean beaters with electric mixer at high speed until stiff but not dry; set aside.

6 Beat egg yolks in separate large bowl with fork. Stir into cornmeal mixture. Stir ⅓ of egg whites into cornmeal mixture to lighten.

7 Fold remaining egg whites into cornmeal mixture until all egg whites are evenly incorporated. Pour into prepared souffle dish.

8 Bake about 50 minutes or until puffed and golden brown. Serve immediately. Garnish, if desired.

Makes 6 servings
*Egg whites must be free from any yolk to reach proper volume when beaten.

Stamped Recipe Cards

WHAT YOU'LL NEED

Tracing paper

Soft-lead pencil

Eraser carving material

Cutting surface or board

Craft knife (#11 blade)

Linoleum cutter (#21 blade)

Ink pads: yellow, red

Scrap paper

12 smooth off-white cards, 4 × 6 inches each

Ruler

Dark green colored pencil

24-inch length dark green raffia

These cards make a terrific gift for anyone who cooks, but save the healthful tart for yourself!♥

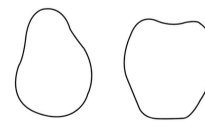

Patterns are 100%.

STEP 1

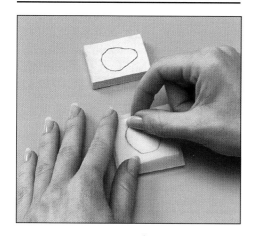

STEP 2

STEP 3

STEP 4

STEP 5

1 Trace pear and apple patterns on page 170, using the pencil, and then transfer them to eraser carving material by placing paper face down and rubbing back of image with your thumbnail.

2 On cutting surface, cut 2 images apart with craft knife, and then cut them out using linoleum cutter. (As you cut, turn carving material rather than moving cutter.) Trim away excess from images with craft knife, slanting cuts away from image.

3 Using red and yellow ink pads, test images by stamping on scrap paper. Trim again if necessary.

4 On each card, stamp pear in yellow at each end and in middle along bottom. Stamp apple in red between pears.

5 Use ruler and dark green pencil to mark off lines ½ inch apart on each card, starting ½ inch from top. If desired, mark off lines on reverse side, as well. Use green pencil to draw in stems and leaves.

6 Bundle cards and tie with raffia.

Autumn Pear Tart

Reduced Fat Pastry (recipe
 follows)
3 to 4 tablespoons sugar
2 tablespoons cornstarch
3 to 4 large pears, cut into
 halves, cored, pared, and
 sliced
1 tablespoon lemon juice
 Ground cinnamon (optional)
 Ground nutmeg (optional)
¼ cup apple jelly, apricot
 spreadable fruit, or honey,
 warm

1 Preheat oven to 425°F. Roll out
pastry on floured surface to
⅛-inch thickness. Ease pastry into
9-inch tart pan; trim edge. Pierce
bottom of pastry with tines of fork;
bake 15 to 20 minutes or until
pastry begins to brown. Cool on
wire rack.

2 Combine sugar and cornstarch
in small bowl; mix well.
Sprinkle pears with lemon juice;
toss with sugar mixture. Arrange
sliced pears on pastry. Sprinkle
lightly with cinnamon and nutmeg,
if desired.

3 Bake 20 to 30 minutes or until
pears are tender and crust is
browned. Cool on wire rack.
Brush pears with jelly. Remove
side of pan; place tart on serving
plate.

Makes 8 servings

REDUCED FAT PASTRY
1⅓ cups cake flour
 2 tablespoons sugar
 ¼ teaspoon salt
 ¼ cup vegetable shortening
 4 to 5 tablespoons ice water

Combine flour, sugar, and salt in
small bowl. Cut in shortening with
pastry blender or two knives until
mixture forms coarse crumbs. Mix
in ice water, 1 tablespoon at a time,
until mixture comes together and
forms a soft dough. Wrap in plastic
wrap. Refrigerate 30 minutes before using.

Makes pastry for one (9-inch) tart

A harvest moon!
And on the mats —
Shadows of pine boughs.

Kikaku
"Harvest Moon"

172

Tommy the Thanksgiving Turkey

WHAT YOU'LL NEED

10 × 13-inch solid brown fabric

10 × 20-inch fall print fabric

2-inch square red fabric

1-inch square yellow fabric

3-inch square fusible webbing

Black fabric paint

2 black beads, 4mm each

10 ounces polyester fiberfill

Hot glue gun, glue sticks

Tommy the Turkey will grace your Thanksgiving table. His whimsical face and colorful tail-feathers make him a fine dinner companion. ♥

STEP 1

STEP 2

STEP 4

STEP 5

STEP 6

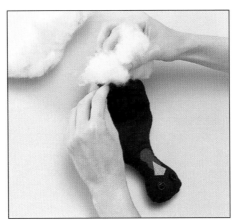

STEP 7

1 Trace turkey head-body on wrong side of brown fabric, trace tailfeathers on wrong side of fall print. Traced lines are seam lines. Cut out ½ inch outside drawn lines.

2 With wrong sides together, stitch tailfeathers together on traced lines, leaving bottom open to turn. Repeat with head-body. Clip curves and points and turn.

3 Following manufacturer's directions, iron fusible webbing to the back of red and yellow fabrics.

4 Trace beak and wattle on paper of fusible webbing. Cut out pieces and remove paper backing. Following manufacturer's directions, fuse beak and wattle to turkey face. Paint eyes on face. When paint dries, stitch on beads for eyes.

5 Stitch lines for tail feathers through both layers.

6 Stuff tail feathers and head-body. Stitch openings closed.

7 Using hot glue gun, glue tail feathers to head-body.

174

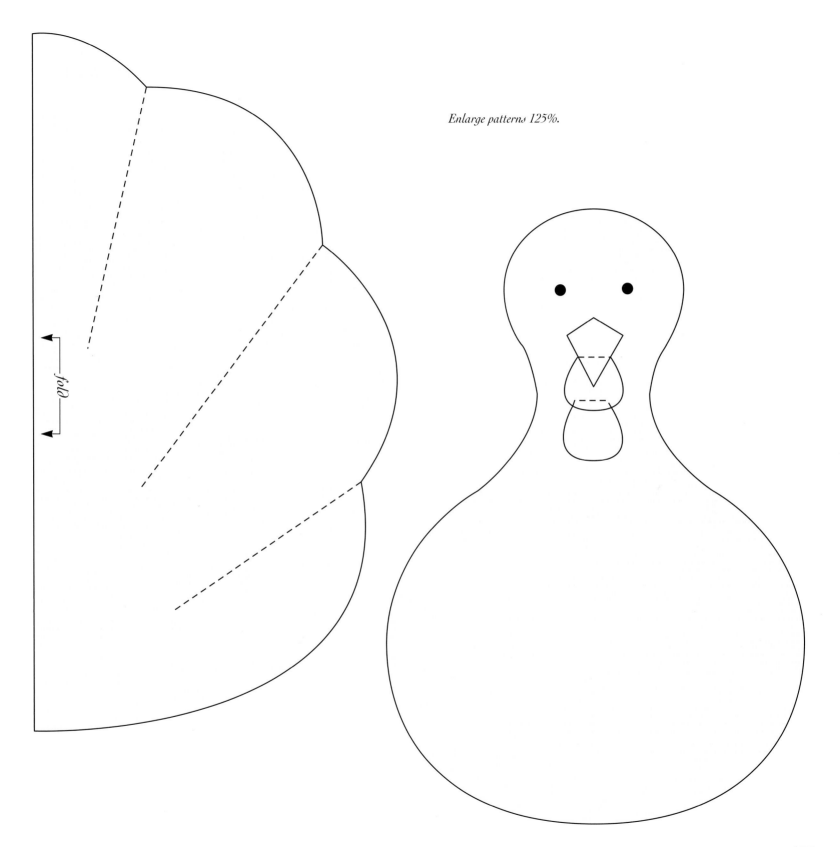

Enlarge patterns 125%.

fold

Roast Turkey with Pan Gravy

♥

*N*o *meal is more American than roast turkey on Thanksgiving, but it's so delicious, treat yourself more than once a year.* ♥

1 fresh or thawed frozen turkey (12 to 14 pounds),* reserve giblets and neck (discard liver or reserve for another use)
Your favorite stuffing (optional)
2 cloves garlic, minced (optional)
½ cup butter, melted
Turkey Broth with Giblets (recipe follows)
1 cup dry white wine or vermouth
3 tablespoons all-purpose flour
Salt and freshly ground black pepper

1 Heat oven to 450°F. Rinse turkey; pat dry with paper towels.

2 Prepare stuffing, if desired. Stuff body and neck cavities loosely with stuffing, if desired.

3 Fold skin over openings and close with skewers. Tie legs together with cotton string or tuck through skin flap, if provided. Tuck wings under turkey.

4 Place turkey on meat rack in shallow roasting pan. If desired, stir garlic into butter. Insert meat thermometer in thickest part of thigh not touching bone. Brush ⅓ of butter mixture evenly over turkey.

5 Place turkey in oven and immediately turn temperature down to 325°F. Roast 18 to 20 minutes per pound for unstuffed turkey or 22 to 24 minutes per pound for stuffed turkey, brushing with butter mixture after 1 hour and then after 1½ hours. Baste with pan juices every hour of roasting. (Total roasting time should be 4 to 5 hours.) If turkey is overbrowning, tent with foil. Turkey is done when internal temperature reaches 180°F and legs move easily in socket.

6 While turkey is roasting, prepare Turkey Broth with Giblets.

7 Transfer turkey to cutting board; tent with foil. Let stand 15 minutes while preparing gravy.

8 Pour off and reserve all juices from roasting pan. To deglaze the pan, pour wine into pan. Place pan over burners and cook over medium-high heat, scraping up browned bits and stirring constantly 2 to 3 minutes or until the mixture has reduced by about half.

9 Spoon off ⅓ cup fat from pan drippings;** discard any remaining fat. Place ⅓ cup fat in large saucepan.

10 Add flour; cook over medium heat 1 minute, stirring constantly. Slowly stir in the 3 cups Turkey Broth with Giblets, the defatted turkey drippings from the roasting pan, and the deglazed wine mixture from roasting pan.

11 Cook over medium heat 10 minutes, stirring occasionally. Stir in reserved chopped giblets; heat through. Season with salt and pepper to taste. Carve turkey with carving knife.

Makes 12 servings and 3½ cups gravy
*A 12- to 14-pound turkey should take 2 to 3 days to thaw in the refrigerator. Do not thaw at room temperature.
**Or, substitute ⅓ cup butter or margarine for turkey fat.
Creamy Turkey Gravy: Stir in 1 cup heavy cream with giblets; proceed as recipe directs. Makes 4½ cups gravy.

TURKEY BROTH WITH GIBLETS

Reserved giblets and neck
    from turkey (discard liver
    or reserve for another use)
4 cups water
1 can (about 14 ounces) chicken
    broth
1 medium onion, cut into
    quarters
2 medium carrots, coarsely
    chopped or sliced
4 large parsley sprigs
1 bay leaf
1 teaspoon dried thyme leaves,
    crushed
10 whole black peppercorns

1 For Turkey Broth, combine turkey giblets and neck, water, and chicken broth in 3-quart saucepan. Bring to a boil over high heat; skim off any foam.

2 Stir in onion, carrots, parsley, bay leaf, thyme, and peppercorns. Reduce heat to low. Simmer, uncovered, 1½ to 2 hours, stirring occasionally. (If liquid evaporates too quickly, add additional ½ cup water.) Cool to room temperature.

3 Strain broth; set aside. If broth measures less than 3 cups, add water to equal 3 cups liquid. If broth measures more than 3 cups, bring to a boil and heat until liquid is reduced to 3 cups.

4 Remove meat from neck and chop giblets finely; set aside.

5 Broth may be prepared up to 1 day before serving. Cover giblets and broth separately and refrigerate. Garnish as desired.

Makes 3 cups

Cornucopia Centerpiece

♥

A beautiful centerpiece for your Thanksgiving table, this cornucopia can be filled with fresh fruit or an assortment of fresh-baked breads or rolls. ♥

INGREDIENTS

1 package (16 ounces) hot roll mix, plus ingredients to prepare mix
2 egg yolks
1 tablespoon cold water
Assorted fresh fruit (optional)

SUPPLIES

1 (16 × 14-inch) piece lightweight cardboard
Tape
Foil

1 To make cornucopia mold, shape cardboard into cone shape. The large open end of cone should measure about 6 inches in diameter. Tape securely. Trim if necessary. Cover outside of cone with foil; grease.

2 Prepare hot roll mix according to package directions. Knead dough on lightly floured surface until smooth, about 5 minutes. Cover loosely; let stand in bowl about 15 minutes.

3 Grease cookie sheet. Set aside ⅛ of dough. Roll and stretch remaining dough on lightly floured surface into triangle. Shape reserved dough into 28- to 30-inch rope (about ½ inch thick).

4 Shape dough triangle around cone, pinching seam on bottom to seal. At point of cornucopia, stretch dough 3 to 4 inches and form a loop, pinching to top of cornucopia to seal.

5 Press dough rope around opening of cornucopia in decorative pattern. Insert wooden toothpicks at 2 inch intervals to hold rope in place during baking. Cover loosely; let rise in warm place until doubled in size, about 30 minutes.

6 Preheat oven to 350°F. Combine egg yolks and water; brush over cornucopia. Bake 20 to 25 minutes or until golden. Remove to wire rack; cool completely. Remove wooden toothpicks. Carefully remove cardboard mold, if desired. Fill with assorted fresh fruit.

Makes 1 cornucopia

Braided Bread Napkin Rings

♥

*H*omemade napkin rings will bring country charm to your holiday table. ♥

INGREDIENTS
   1 package (16 ounces) hot roll
      mix, plus ingredients to
      prepare mix
   1 egg yolk
   1 tablespoon cold water

SUPPLIES
   4 paper tubes from paper
      towels, foil, or other wrap
   Foil

1 Wrap tubes in foil; grease lightly. Grease baking sheets.

2 Prepare hot roll mix according to package directions. Knead dough on floured surface until smooth. Cover loosely; let stand in bowl about 15 minutes.

3 Roll dough on lightly floured surface into two 12 × 6-inch rectangles. Cut dough into 48 (6 × ½ inch) strips.

4 Braid 3 strips of dough. Wrap around prepared tubes, pinching ends of dough to seal. Repeat with remaining dough. Place on prepared baking sheets. Cover loosely; let rise until double in size, about 30 minutes.

5 Preheat oven to 375°F. Combine egg yolk and water; carefully brush on dough.

6 Bake 10 to 12 minutes or until golden. Remove tubes to wire racks; cool completely on tubes. Carefully remove rings.

Makes 16 napkin rings

Note: If making less than 16 napkin rings, remaining dough can be shaped into rolls and baked according to package directions.

Golden Leaf Pumpkin Pie

*S*infully rich and perfectly spiced, this pumpkin pie is topped with a pile of golden-glazed leaves. ♥

1 package (15 ounces) refrigerated pie crust, divided
1 can (16 ounces) solid pack pumpkin
1 cup half-and-half
3 eggs
⅔ cup sugar
¼ cup honey
2 teaspoons ground cinnamon
1 teaspoon ground allspice
1 teaspoon ground nutmeg
½ teaspoon ground ginger
½ teaspoon ground cloves
½ teaspoon salt
Golden Leaves (recipe follows)

Pattern is 100%.

1 Preheat oven to 425°F.

2 Roll 1 pie crust on floured surface into 10-inch circle; ease into 9-inch pie plate. Trim and flute. Reserve remaining pie crust for Golden Leaves.

3 Combine remaining ingredients except Golden Leaves. Pour into crust.

4 Bake 10 minutes. Reduce oven temperature to 350°F. Bake 40 to 45 minutes until pastry is brown and knife inserted in center comes out clean. Cool. Garnish with Golden Leaves. Refrigerate leftovers.

Makes 8 to 10 servings

GOLDEN LEAVES
1 refrigerated pie crust, reserved from pie
½ cup half-and-half
3 tablespoons sugar

1 Roll pastry on floured surface to ⅛-inch thickness. Using diagram as a guide, cut out leaf shapes. Mark veins in leaves with tip of knife. Roll pastry scraps into rope ¼-inch thick. Cut into 2- to 3-inch pieces and make tendrils.

2 Preheat oven to 400°F. Lay pastry leaves on bottom of inverted flat-bottomed ovenproof bowl so that leaves curve.* Lay tendrils on ungreased baking sheet. Brush leaves and tendrils with half-and-half; sprinkle with sugar. Bake 10 to 15 minutes or until golden brown. Remove to wire rack; cool completely.

Makes about 12 leaves
*Leaves may also be baked flat on ungreased baking sheet.

Halloween Sweatshirt

♥

Black sweatshirt

Iron, ironing board

See-through ruler

½ yard light fusible webbing

12 × 9-inch piece black/rust mini-check fabric

12 × 9-inch piece rust/black plaid fabric

12 × 9-inch piece tan/beige mini-check fabric

Embroidery floss: rust, black

Embroidery needle

Scraps: mustard calico (moon), black calico (bat, pumpkin face, cat), orange calico (pumpkin), green calico (leaf), brown calico (stem)

Tracing paper, pencil

Thread to match calico, plaid, and checked fabrics

Fabric glue

18 buttons, various shapes and sizes

Homespun patches make this ordinary sweatshirt festive. ♥

184

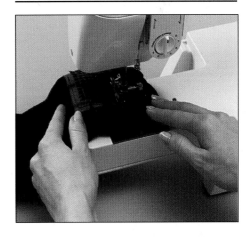

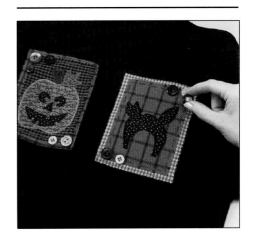

1 Iron 6½ × 5-inch sections of fusible webbing to the black/rust mini-check, rust/black plaid, and tan/beige fabrics. Remove paper backings. Tear a 4 × 5½-inch square from each piece.

2 Tear a 3½ × 5-inch square from unfused portions of fabrics (these have not been fused with webbing) listed in Step 1. Place small tan/beige square on top of large black/rust mini-check square, place small black/rust mini-check square on top of large rust/black plaid square, and place small rust/black plaid on top of large tan/beige square. Using 6 strands of rust floss, stitch a long running stitch around each small piece to secure it to bottom piece.

3 Fuse scraps of webbing to back of scrap pieces of fabric for shapes. Remove paper. Trace patterns onto paper backing.

4 Position moon and bat on first square, pumpkin with face, leaf, and stem on second square, and cat on third square. Fuse in place. Position squares on center front of sweatshirt and fuse.

5 Using an appliqué stitch and matching thread, stitch around each design. Use black floss to stitch whiskers on cat.

6 With scraps leftover from the plaids or mini-check fabrics, cut 2 squares 2½ × 2½ inches and 2 squares out of another fabric 2 × 2 inches. Place the smaller on top of the larger, and stitch around the edges following instructions in Step 2. Place a square on each sleeve and straight stitch around edges.

7 On front squares, glue buttons in each corner. For squares on sleeves, glue 3 buttons to center of each. Let glue dry overnight.

Patterns are 100%.

Glazed Stuffed Pork Chops

♥

1 Chop 6 apple quarters; reserve remaining 2 quarters. Combine chopped apples, slaw blend, raisins, ¼ cup apple cider, syrup, and 2 teaspoons mustard in large saucepan. Cover and cook over medium heat 5 minutes or until cabbage is tender.

2 Make a pocket in each pork chop by cutting horizontally through chop almost to bone. Fill each pocket with about ¼ cup apple mixture. Keep remaining apple mixture warm.

3 Spray nonstick skillet with cooking spray. Heat over medium heat. Brown pork chops about 3 minutes on each side. Add ¼ cup apple cider. Reduce heat; cover and simmer 8 minutes or until pork is barely pink in center. Remove from skillet; keep warm.

4 Add liquid from remaining apple mixture to skillet. Combine remaining ¼ cup apple cider, 2 teaspoons mustard, and cornstarch; stir until smooth. Stir into skillet. Simmer over medium heat until thickened. Spoon glaze over chops and apple mixture. Slice remaining 2 apple quarters; divide between servings. Garnish if desired.

Makes 2 servings

2 medium cooking apples, quartered
3 cups prepared cabbage slaw blend
¼ cup raisins
¾ cup apple cider, divided
2 tablespoons maple-flavored pancake syrup

4 teaspoons spicy brown mustard, divided
2 lean pork chops (about 6 ounces each), 1 inch thick
Nonstick cooking spray
2 teaspoons cornstarch

Zucchini Chow Chow

♥

2 cups thinly sliced zucchini
2 cups thinly sliced yellow
    summer squash*
½ cup thinly sliced red onion
    Salt
1½ cups cider vinegar
1 to 1¼ cups sugar
1½ tablespoons pickling spice
1 cup thinly sliced carrots
1 small red bell pepper, thinly
    sliced

1. Sprinkle zucchini, summer squash, and onion lightly with salt; let stand in colander 30 minutes. Rinse well with cold water; drain thoroughly. Pat dry with paper towels.

2. Combine vinegar, sugar, and pickling spice in medium saucepan. Bring to a boil over high heat. Add carrots and bell pepper; bring to a boil. Remove from heat; cool to room temperature.

3. Spoon zucchini, summer squash, onion, and carrot mixture into sterilized jars; cover and refrigerate up to 3 weeks.

Makes 24 (1 cup) servings
*If yellow summer squash is not available, increase zucchini to 4 cups.

Tie a ribbon around the jar for a perfect gift with lots of country charm. ♥

Fall Harvest Wreath

♥

WHAT YOU'LL NEED

18-inch grapevine wreath

Hot glue gun, glue sticks

6 stems silk green grape ivy

3 stems silk reddish brown grape ivy, each with 2 bunches of grapes

3 to 4 dried pomegranates

10 to 12 dried assorted zinnia and black-eyed Susan heads

8 stems dried green hydrangea

Wire cutters

A feast for the eyes, this wreath is embellished with grapes, pomegranates, hydrangeas, zinnias, and ivy. The rich and deep fall colors will add an inviting warmth to your home.♥

1 Hot glue green and reddish brown grape ivy around grapevine wreath.

2 Hot glue pomegranates and flower heads randomly around wreath in a circular design.

3 Hot glue hydrangea stems into the open areas of the grapevine wreath following the circular contour of wreath.

TIP
Try using dried mini corn or dried gourds on your fall harvest wreath. Drop some cinnamon scented oils onto the wreath to add a special autumn fragrance.

Seasons of mists and mellow fruitfulness,
Close bosom-friend of the maturing sun.

John Keats
"To Autumn"

SOURCES FOR PRODUCTS

Most of the craft materials used in the projects in this book, such as brushes, paints, fusible webbing, or tapes, are available at craft, hobby, or fabric stores nationwide. Other products may give equally good results. Specialized products that are specific to a project are listed below by page number; these products are also widely available. For further information, contact the manufacturers at the addresses given at the bottom of the page.

Page 20: Kunin felt: Foss Manufacturing Co. **Page 26:** Wonder Under transfer webbing: Freudenberg Nonwovens. **Page 34:** Americana acrylic paint (Buttermilk, Ebony Black, Country Red): DecoArt. Folk Art acrylic paint (Green Meadow): Plaid Enterprises, Inc. **Page 42:** Birch wreath: Colorado Birch Products. Preserved greens: Mirsky, Inc. Silk cranberries: Winward Silks. **Page 46:** Rit tan dye: RIT. Warm & Natural cotton batting: Warm Products, Inc. Poly-fil: Fairfield Processing Corp. **Page 50:** Large Cloud Home birdhouse: Walnut Hollow. Weathered Wood crackle: DecoArt. **Page 52:** Wood sealer, Americana acrylic paint (Burnt Umber, Buttermilk, Country Red, Ebony Black, Pumpkin,

Flesh Tone), Wood'N Resin oak gel stain: DecoArt. Folk Art acrylic paint (Green Meadow): Plaid Enterprises, Inc. **Page 57:** RIT tan dye: RIT. Warm & Natural cotton batting: Warm Products, Inc. Wonder Under transfer webbing: Freudenberg Nonwovens. Poly-fil: Fairfield Processing Corp. Velcro hook-and-loop tape: Velcro. **Page 74:** Folk Art acrylic paint (Bluegrass, Raspberry Sherbert, Victorian Rose, Blue Satin, Spring Rose): Plaid Enterprises, Inc. Accent acrylic paint (Indian Sky, Stoneware Blue, Sedona Clay): Accent Products Division. Americana acrylic paint (Snow White, Mink Tan, Buttermilk): DecoArt. Ceramcoat acrylic paint (Black): Delta Technical Coatings, Inc. **Page 80:** Aleene's OK to Wash It fabric glue: Aleene's, Division of Artis, Inc. Battenburg doilies: Wimpole Street Creations. **Page 85:** Pillow: Adam Originals. Embroidery floss: The DMC Corp. **Page 90:** Pellon fleece batting: Freudenberg Nonwovens. **Page 94:** Birdhouse, post: Flowerfields & Co. Honeysuckle vine: Red River Vine Co. **Page 98:** Roses & Ribbon Terra-Cotta container: Bloomrite Brand Nurserymens Exchange. Dried flowers: Mirsky, Inc. **Page 101:** Kunin felt: Foss Manufacturing Company. Embroidery floss: The DMC Corp.

Silk ribbon: YLI Corporation. Pellon Stitch-N-Tear tear-away: Freudenberg Nonwovens. **Page 106:** Antique watering can: Woodchip MFG and Distribution. Dried flowers: Mirsky, Inc. **Page 123:** Embroidery floss: The DMC Corp. Linen (28-count): Wichelt Imports, Inc. **Page 127:** Plastic canvas: Darice Manufacturing. Needleloft plastic canvas yarn: Uniek, Inc. Embroidery floss: The DMC Corp. **Page 135:** Kunin felt: Foss Manufacturing Co. Embroidery floss: The DMC Corp. **Page 138:** Herb rack: Woodchip MFG and Distribution. Dried flowers: Mirsky, Inc. **Page 142:** RIT tan dye: RIT. Poly-fil: Fairfield Processing Corp. **Page 152:** Bag: Adams Originals. Embroidery floss: The DMC Corp. **Page 163:** HeatnBond UltraHold fusible webbing, vinyl: Therm O Web. **Page 173:** Wonder Under transfer webbing: Freudenberg Nonwovens. Poly-fil: Fairfield Processing Corp. **Page 184:** HeatnBond Lite fusible webbing: Therm O Web. Creatively Yours Crafters Cement glue: Loctite Corp. Embroidery floss: The DMC Corp. **Page 189:** Dried flowers: Mirsky, Inc. Silk greens: Winward Silks.

Adams Originals
7471 Lamar Ave. South
Cottage Grove, MN 55016

Aleene's
Division of Artis, Inc.
Buellton, CA 93427

Accent Products Division
300 East Main St.
Lake Zurich, IL 60047

Bloomrite Brand Nurserymens Exchange
475 6th St.
San Francisco, CA 94103

Colorado Birch Products
3563 Walnut
Denver, CO 80205

The DMC Corporation
10 Port Kearny
South Kearny, NJ 07032

DecoArt
P.O. Box 360
Stanford, KY 40484

Darice Manufacturing
21160 Drake Rd.
Strongsville, OH 44136-6699

Fairfield Processing Corp.
P.O. Drawer 1157
Danbury, CT 06810

Flowerfields & Co.
131 Standish
Schaumburg, IL 60193

Foss Manufacturing Company
380 Lafayette Road
P.O. 5000
Hampton, NH 03843-5000

Freudenberg Nonwovens
Pellon Division
1040 Avenue of the Americas
New York, NY 10018

Loctite Corporation
705 N. Mountain Rd.
Newington, CT 06111

Mirsky, Inc.
P.O. Box 874
Beaverton, OR 97075

Plaid Enterprises, Inc.
1649 International Blvd.
Norcross, GA 30093

Red River Vine Co.
831 E. Broad
Texarkana, TX 75502

RIT Consumer Affairs Dept. DP-1
P.O. Box 21070
Indianapolis, IN 46221

Stearns Technical Textiles Co.
100 Williams St.
Cincinnati, OH 45215-4683

Sulky Decorative Threads
3113 Broadpoint Dr.
Harbor Heights, FL 33983

Thermo O Web
770 Glenn Ave.
Wheeling, IL 60090

Uniek, Inc.
805 Uniek Dr.
P.O. Box 457
Waunakee, WI 53597-0457

Velcro USA Inc.
406 Brown Ave.
Manchester, NH 03103

Warm Products, Inc.
16110 Woodinville
Redmond Rd. #4
Woodinville, WA 98072

Walnut Hollow
Route 1, Hwy. 23 North
Dodgeville, WI 53533

Wimpole Street Creations
P.O. Box 395
West Bountiful, UT 84087

Wichelt Imports, Inc.
Box 139, Hwy. 35
Stoddard, WI 54658

Winward Silks
30063 Ahern Ave.
Union City, CA 94587

Woodchip MFG and Distribution
P.O. Box 59
DuQuoin, IL 62832

YLI Corporation
482 N. Freedom Blvd.
Provo, UT 84601

FOOD INDEX

CRAFT INDEX